JENNINGS TO THE RESCUE

Also by Anthony Buckeridge:

THE 'JENNINGS' BOOKS
JENNINGS SOUNDS THE ALARM – Radio plays 1-7
JENNINGS BREAKS THE RECORD – Radio plays 8-14
JENNINGS JOINS THE SEARCH PARTY – Radio plays 15-20
JENNINGS AND THE ROMAN REMAINS – Radio plays 27-32

THE 'REX MILLIGAN' BOOKS
INTRODUCING REX MILLIGAN – the uncollected stories
A FUNNY THING HAPPENED

A Musical for Schools:
JENNINGS ABOUNDING

Autobiography:
WHILE I REMEMBER

Related reading:
THE JENNINGS COMPANION by David Bathurst

JENNINGS

TO THE RESCUE

Plays for radio – volume 4

by

Anthony Buckeridge

with illustrations by Val Biro

DS

David Schutte

Text copyright © Anthony Buckeridge 1950, 1951, 2002

Illustrations copyright © Val Biro 2002

First published in 2002
by DAVID SCHUTTE
119 Sussex Road, Petersfield, Hampshire GU31 4LB

Illustrations by Val Biro

ISBN 0 9521482 5 0

A CIP catalogue record for this book
is available from the British Library

Typesetting by KT
Printed in the U.K. by
Polestar AUP Aberdeen Limited

CONTENTS

ILLUSTRATIONS

INTRODUCTION

This is the year of my father's 90th birthday and on looking back I realise how privileged I am to have been part of the Jennings phenomenon for over fifty years. As children, my sister Sally and I took it all very much for granted. Dad would be in his office writing yet another new Jennings book but we never knew very much about it, nothing about the plots, nor even the title. We would have to wait for it to be published before we could find out.

We were both quietly proud of him when people recognised our surname and asked if we were any relation to Anthony Buckeridge. But now as adults we are enormously proud of him for what he has achieved in bringing laughter and happiness to generations of Jennings readers across the world and for his contribution to children's literature. My father has said of his writing, "What I do is start with a real life situation and take it just one step further."

Many of the stories do have real life connections, but in reality most children's escapades are either nipped in the bud by an adult not wanting events to get out of hand, or they just run out of steam of their own accord. By allowing them to develop that 'one step further' a whole new dimension appears as Father's imagination takes control of events and the story line takes on a new lease of life and a new direction.

I am happy to recall that some of my activities as a child and as an adult have found their way into the Jennings books. For example, in the late forties we lived in a flat at Ramsgate overlooking the harbour and enjoyed watching the French fishing boats which sheltered in the port during bad weather. Before they set off to sea again my sister and I would walk along the harbour wall and watch the fishermen get ready to sail. It was on one of these occasions that Sally decided she would like to obtain a couple of the green glass buoyancy floats that the fishermen used on their nets. As neither of us spoke sufficient French, and both of us lacking the courage to go up and ask, we decided that Dad should do the deed for us. We returned home, explained the problem, and a few minutes later we were off again to the harbour with Dad armed with a couple of packets of Woodbines as barter! He conversed with the crew of the fishing boat and we were soon the proud owners of two green glass floats, each with its own beautiful protective rope plaiting.

I admit that this is no great story but it was obviously sufficient to set the thought processes in motion for Dad to work on. The end result was the wonderful story in the radio play *Jennings and the Unwelcome Gift* (5th February 1949) later adapted for the book *Jennings and Darbishire* (1952) where the two boys meet the crew of a French fishing boat sheltering in Linbury Cove. It is a great example of taking a real life situation that 'one step further'.

Many years (and numerous incidents) later I was working on a farm in Surrey and became involved in helping to run the village fête. I volunteered to run a 'bowling for the pig' stall, and on the day I took along a small piglet as a form of visual attraction. The afternoon passed without too much excitement and the eventual winner was a senior citizen gentleman who lived in a high rise block of flats in Redhill!! It was never intended for my piglet to be the prize – this pensioner won a large joint of pork and the runner-up received a few pounds of pork sausages. A few weeks later I mentioned the events of the fête to my father, and he seemed mildly amused by the story, and then somewhat preoccupied in thought, but I thought nothing more of it! The following year the new Jennings book (*Jennings in Particular*, 1968) had a dust jacket which depicted Mr Wilkins enmeshed in the cricket nets whilst attempting to catch a small piglet! With his over-active imagination, Father had held on to the image of my village fête story, worked on the content somewhat ('one step further') so that it was Jennings who won a real pig at the Linbury parish fête, and all the consequences that went with it!

Few modern authors can claim to have had their work in print for over fifty years so this surely must place Jennings in the category of 'classic', for a classic must be able to withstand the test of time, and the Jennings books have certainly achieved this requirement.

So, with your copy of this fourth volume of the Radio Scripts series, sit back, relax and enjoy.

Tim Buckeridge
March 2002

PUBLISHER's NOTE

The letters that precede each play in the present volume were letters written by Jennings to David Davis, the producer of *Children's Hour*, as a prelude to each episode of *Jennings at School*. The letters were broadcast as advertising trailers for each play, read out on air by David Davis himself, usually each Monday, when he was announcing the programme schedules for the forthcoming week. They were used only once, and are now published for the first time.

Linbury Court Preparatory School

Dear David,

I expect you are glad because I have not written to you for a long time, to hear from me now. I expect you will be surprised to know that although nothing ever happens at school like serious crime, as you probably think, sometimes something does happen as I shall tell you. And it all proves that when Mr Wilkins punishes you unfairly for doing a famous off-drive with a blackboard duster which wasn't really your fault, and then goes off to enjoy himself at the match - well that sort of thing is not cricket; though as it happened the match was cricket as it was last term that it happened.

I must stop now as I have no blotch, so can't turn over, but will tell you all about it on Wed.

Yours affeckly, J.C.T. Jennings.
P.S. Darbishire says not to forget that he wants to be remembered.

JENNINGS
WATCHES THE MATCH

(Fourth series no.1)

Jennings Watches the Match was the twenty-first Jennings play.

It was first broadcast by the BBC Home Service for Children's Hour on 10th October 1951 with the following cast:

JENNINGS	John Charlesworth
DARBISHIRE	Henry Searle
VENABLES	Bill Croydon
TEMPLE	Lance Secretan
ATKINSON	Robin Netscher
MR. CARTER	Geoffrey Wincott
MR. WILKINS	Wilfred Babbage
MR. FINDLATER }	
SHADY CHARACTER }	Roger Snowdon

Produced by David Davis

ANNOUNCER: This is the BBC Home Service. Hullo children.

Music

Jennings at School. The last we heard from Jennings was at the end of the spring term when he and Darbishire, Temple, Venables, Atkinson and the rest of them were on their way home, leaving Mr Carter, Mr Wilkins, Matron and the other grown-ups mopping their brows and wondering how they could ever face another term of it at Linbury Court School. However, they seem to have managed it, and our new series of Jennings adventures which starts today takes us to somewhere in the middle of the summer term, with the cricket season at its height.

Cross fade music to Jennings, humming. Fade in distant background of voices and footsteps. Jennings stops humming and calls.

JENNINGS: I say, Venables, what's all the excitement about?

VENABLES: (*distant and approaching, with footsteps*) Out of my way, Jennings. Don't block up the corridor. Can't you see I'm in a hurry?

JENNINGS: Yes, but what's up – place on fire, or ship sinking?

VENABLES: Don't ask me: all I know is I've got to get a move on. Look, if you don't move that bottle of bat oil off the floor, you'll get it knocked over.

JENNINGS: Surely a chap can oil his cricket bat in peace? Where are you going, anyway?

VENABLES: I don't really know till I get there, but I'm wizard-well going to be first on the scene when I find out where it is. Can't stop now. Operation Rush-Hour.

Exclamation from Jennings as bottle falls over

Oh, sorry, Jen: there goes your bat oil.

JENNINGS: You great clumsy bazooka, Venables. You've spilt the whole bottle full, slap-bang-doyng all over the floor.

VENABLES: (*going*) Super sorrow! But I'll pick it up later – can't stop now. Urgent.

JENNINGS: Hey, come back and help me... Oh, gosh, you are a cad, beetling off like that.

TEMPLE: (*off, approaching*) Jennings! – I say, Jennings, have you seen Venables anywhere around these parts?

JENNINGS: I should wizard-well think I have, Temple. That's why my bat oil's been knocked for six all over the corridor.

TEMPLE: Oh, good – I mean, hard luck! Where's Venables going?

JENNINGS: He doesn't know till he gets there.

TEMPLE: All right, I'll find him. Oh, yes, and if Atkinson ankles along, tell him I've gone to look for Venables, who's gone to look for the excitement.

JENNINGS: Yes: but what *is* the excitement?

TEMPLE: I don't know. Mr. Wilkins was coming down the stairs behind me. You'd better ask him. (*Fading*) I say, look at all this bat oil all over the shop! You are a clumsy hippopotamus, Jennings, turning the place into a skating rink just when everyone's in a supersonic hurry.

JENNINGS: Well! I like that! Hey, wait for me and I'll... Oh, sir, sir! Mr. Wilkins, please sir, what's all the excitement about, sir?

MR. WILKINS: (*approaching*) Excitement! What excitement? I don't look unusually excited, do I?

JENNINGS: Oh, no, I don't mean you, so to speak, personally, sir. That is, not you, as it were, yourself, sir.

MR. WILKINS: Not as what was myself? I don't know what you're talking about. I'm feeling quite myself, thank you.

JENNINGS: No, what I meant was, sir...

MR. WILKINS: Good gracious: just look at this bat oil spilt all over the corridor! Is that your oil, Jennings?

JENNINGS: Yes, sir.

MR. WILKINS: I might have known it: whenever something happens that shouldn't happen, it's always your fault.

JENNINGS: Oh, no, sir, honestly it isn't mine, sir.

MR. WILKINS: Not yours! But, you silly little boy, you just said it was.

JENNINGS: Oh, yes, the oil is, sir, but the fault isn't: or rather, I didn't actually spill it myself, personally, as you might say.

MR. WILKINS: I might say a lot of things, Jennings: but what I am saying is that the Pavilion's the place for cricket gear, and if I see that bat indoors again, I shall confiscate it.

JENNINGS: Yes, sir.

MR. WILKINS: And now mop up the oil on the floor.

JENNINGS: Yes, sir; with my handkerchief, sir?

MR. WILKINS: No, no, you silly little boy, of course not with your handkerchief. Use a rag. Where's the rag you were oiling your bat with?

JENNINGS: Here, sir, only – well this *is* my handkerchief that I was using, sir.

MR. WILKINS: I... I... I... corwumph! Now look here, Jennings...

13

MR. CARTER: (*slight approach*) Excuse me, Mr. Wilkins, may I come by?

MR. WILKINS: Oh, it's you, is it Carter? Yes, of course you can, but watch your step. This wretched boy has just flooded the narrowest part of the corridor with bat oil.

MR. CARTER: Pity. I expect he was a bit excited: they all are at the moment. They're waiting for me to pin this notice on the board.

MR. WILKINS: Which notice is that?

MR. CARTER: It's about the whole holiday tomorrow. We're taking the first and second elevens and scorers to the County Cricket Ground to see the second day of the Sussex and Middlesex match.

JENNINGS: Oo, *sir*. County cricket! Oh, super-wizzo-sonic!

MR. CARTER: We're hiring a special bus to pick us up at half-past ten. I'm on my way to pin up the announcement now.

JENNINGS: Golly, how socko! I must go and tell Darbishire: he'll be as pleased as a guinea-pig with one tail. (*Going*) Eee-ow-ow... Eee-ow-ow...

MR. WILKINS: Hey, Jennings, come back! What about this bottle of...? Well, what do you think of that, Carter! The wretched boy's gone off leaving a pool of bat oil as deep as the Slough of Despond, all over the corridor. I've a good mind not to let him go to the match tomorrow, and if I find one more example of...

Cross fade to Jennings

JENNINGS: Eee-ow-ow... Eee-ow-ow!

Door opens/shuts

Oh, there you are, Darbishire. I say, what do you think? We're going to the County Cricket match tomorrow.

DARBISHIRE: What!! Golly – how super-socko-sonic! I can take my autograph book with me, can't I? I've got six pink pages left specially blank for sporting characters.

JENNINGS: Try and get R.J.Findlater's autograph then. He's bound to be playing. You ought to see his smashing off-drives. He stands like this, look, and then steps forward and hits out... Give me a bowl with the blackboard duster and I'll show you.

DARBISHIRE: But we can't play cricket here in the classroom, so stop waving that cricket bat round your head like a battle-axe. Old Wilkie or someone might come in.

JENNINGS: Just one bowl: I won't hit it hard. You see, I've been modelling my off-drives on R.J.Findlater lately and I can do it wizardly. Tie the blackboard duster in a knot – then you'll be able to chuck it.

DARBISHIRE: Righto – (*going*) gosh, it's terribly chalky. Shouldn't think it's been shaken out since the Stone Age.

JENNINGS: I'll shake it out with my famous beefy-off-drive. (*going*) I'll stand over here. Right – now!

DARBISHIRE: Okay! Coming down then. Pla-ay. (*Door opens*) Oh, good shot, Jennings! Wizard swipe! Oh – oh, golly.

MR. WILKINS: Jennings! I... I... corwumph! (*Splutters and coughs*)

JENNINGS: (*at mic*) Oh, sir, I'm terribly sorry. I didn't mean to hit you with the duster. Honestly, it was an accident, sir.

MR. WILKINS: I... I... what on earth do you think you're doing? You deliberately knocked this chalker full of dusty rag – this duster full of chalky chalk dust *in my face*!

JENNINGS: I didn't mean it, sir. You opened the door just as I was...

DARBISHIRE: Shall I brush you down, sir? You're a bit white round the shoulders.

MR. WILKINS: Gross insolence and rank disobedience. I came to find you, Jennings, because you left the corridor swimming knee-deep in oil. I warned you that if I found you using a cricket bat indoors I should confiscate it. And now here are the two of you deliberately playing cricket in the classroom and bombarding me with chalky dusters full of dusty chalk dust.

DARBISHIRE: We're terribly sorry, sir.

MR. WILKINS: Be quiet, Darbishire. Give me that bat, Jennings. I'll look after this for the rest of the term. And now I'll set you both an imposition to be done tomorrow morning. English Grammar Book – exercises 5, 6 and 7. Pick out the objects and complements in all those sentences.

JENNINGS: Tomorrow morning, sir? Oh, but, sir, not tomorrow morning! We're going to watch the County Cricket tomorrow, sir.

MR. WILKINS: You *were* going to watch the cricket, I understand, but that was before you chose to play indoor cricket instead. So you can start these exercises after breakfast and bring the work to me as soon as it's finished.

JENNINGS: But, sir, that means we can't go at all, sir. We shan't have got them nearly finished by the time the bus comes.

MR. WILKINS: That, Jennings, is one of the things you should have thought of before you broke out into this wave of juvenile delinquency, and took to playing test matches in the classroom. I'll see the work as soon as it's done, and in any case not later than lunch time tomorrow.

Fade out/music/fade in

JENNINGS: Phew! That's the last exercise finished, thank goodness. Have you finished yours, Darbi?

DARBISHIRE: Yes, I've just done the last one. But what are we going to do now, Jen? It's eleven o'clock now and the bus went half an hour ago. *And* Mr. Wilkins went with it, don't forget! I reckon it's jolly unfair going off and enjoying himself and leaving us here doing sentences with objects and complements and things.

JENNINGS: That's why he did it. The object of an unfair sentence like the one he gave us was so that he could go off and leave us behind with his compliments, and what's more... I say, Darbi – he said we'd got to take him these exercises as soon as we'd done them; and in any case before lunch – or else – didn't he?

DARBISHIRE: Yes, but we can't: he's gone to the match.

JENNINGS: Well, that means we can go too, now we've finished. In fact, we've simply *got* to or we shan't be able to show Old Wilkie these exercises before lunch, as he told us to.

DARBISHIRE: Gosh, yes, of course. But it's about ten miles. How can we get there?

JENNINGS: We could hitch-hike. We're bound to get a lift if we flap our fingers at all the cars that come along. Come on; put your exercise book in your pocket. Old Wilkie can correct them this afternoon during the match; he'll enjoy that!

DARBISHIRE: Righto... (*going*) Oh! Just a mo' and I'll get my autograph book: I can't go without that; it's in my desk. (*Desk lid bangs shut*) (*Back*) Here it is – six blank pink pages. I'll try and get all the signatures of both teams – especially that chap who does all those super off-drives you were demonstrating yesterday. What did you say his name was?

JENNINGS: R.J.Findlater – but I doubt if he could do them with a blackboard duster. Let's hurry or we shan't get there before the lunch interval.

DARBISHIRE: *Oh, good shot, Jennings! Wizard swipe! Oh – oh, golly.*

Fade out / music
Fade in car whizzing by without stopping

DARBISHIRE: This is hopeless, Jennings. We've come about a hundred miles already, and none of the cars have even looked like stopping.

JENNINGS: Perhaps they don't understand what we want.

DARBISHIRE: They must be stark raving bats, then. I've jerked both my thumbs out of their sockets, and nearly flapped my hand off at the wrist, and the only thing that's stopped is that old hay-cart.

JENNINGS: And that was going the wrong way! I think he only pulled up because you were frightening the horse.

DARBISHIRE: Well, we must persevere, I suppose. My father says that "if at first you don't succeed..."

Car distant

JENNINGS: There's another one coming now.

DARBISHIRE: What! A hay-cart?

JENNINGS: No, you ruin: one of those supersonic jobs with a radiator like a mouth organ. Wave your autograph book at it.

DARBISHIRE: All right; it's worth having a bash, I suppose.

Car approaches and stops behind speech: hold engine under

JENNINGS: Wizzo, it's stopping! (*Going*) Come on, Darbi: there'll be bags of room. There's only the driver in it... (*Approach*) Excuse me, but would you kindly give us a lift, please?

FINDLATER: Jump in the back then, quickly, I'm in rather a hurry.

JENNINGS: Oh, thank you so much.

FINDLATER: Mind the cricket gear on the floor.

JENNINGS: Yes, of course. Hop in, Darbi.

DARBISHIRE: No, after you, Jennings.

JENNINGS: No, you first. (*They argue amicably*)

FINDLATER: Oi! Oi! Make up your mind: I'm in a hurry.

JENNINGS: Right. Come on then, Darbi. All right, sir.

FINDLATER: Good.

Car door opens/shuts. Car starts: hold engine under

DARBISHIRE: This is very kind of you, sir. We missed the bus, you see. It wouldn't wait while we did our exercises.

FINDLATER: I see. But if you're all that keen on exercise, why not walk the whole way?

JENNINGS: Oh, not that sort of exercise: ours were the other sort – with complements.

FINDLATER: Oh, I see. So that's why you were so polite to each other when you were getting in.

Laughter from Jennings and Darbishire,
though they don't see the point

Now, where do you want me to drop you? I'm going to the County Cricket Ground.

JENNINGS: Oh! We're going there, too. Isn't that smashing? We would have gone with the others, only – I say, excuse me, but I think I've seen you before. You aren't *playing* in the match, are you?

FINDLATER: I am: and I'm very late. I had a puncture a few miles back or I would have been there some time ago. Fortunately we're batting this morning and I'm going in number five, so I'm not likely to be wanted just yet.

JENNINGS: I *knew* I'd seen you before – it was at Lords – against the M.C.C. You're Mr. R.J.Findlater, aren't you?

FINDLATER: Quite correct. And you?

JENNINGS: I'm Jennings, and this is Darbishire. We play cricket too, you know, but I don't suppose you ever heard of us, though. I'm in the Linbury Court second eleven and Darbishire's the scorer.

FINDLATER: How do you do?

JENNINGS: Well, go on, Darbi – say something. Don't sit there and gape like a stuffed mattress. Haven't you ever met any famous sporting characters before?

DARBISHIRE: Oh, yes: I was just thinking what a strange thing it was that Mr. Findlater should give us a lift, because it was all through him that we missed the bus.

FINDLATER: All through me! And what did I do, pray?

JENNINGS: It wasn't really your fault. You needn't blame yourself too much. But I was showing Darbishire how you do your famous off-drives with a chalky duster, and one of the masters came in and caught it, full toss, on the nose.

FINDLATER: Too bad.

DARBISHIRE: It was a good swipe, though. I say, Mr. Findlater, will you sign my autograph book, please? I've got six special pink pages left blank for you.

FINDLATER: I can't do it while we're going at sixty miles an hour. Let me have the book when we get there.

20

DARBISHIRE: I'll slip it in your cricket bag, shall I?

FINDLATER: All right.

DARBISHIRE: There: now you won't forget. And perhaps you'd even ask the rest of the players to sign, too?

JENNINGS: Oh, gosh! I've just thought of something. Would you mind stopping, Mr. Findlater? I've just remembered. We haven't got any money. Mr. Carter's buying tickets for everyone else, but he won't get any for us.

DARBISHIRE: Oh, why didn't we think of that before? It's always little things like that, that bish up the wizardest of schemes. My father says that –

"For want of a nail, a shoe was lost:

For want of a shoe a ..."

JENNINGS: Don't talk such bosh, Darbishire. Nails wouldn't help, even if we'd got any: nor shoes, either. They only take *money* at the pay-box, and if you start offering them a pair of old mouldy ...

FINDLATER: Perhaps I can solve the difficulty. You can come in with me, if you like.

JENNINGS: Oh, but we couldn't let you pay for us.

FINDLATER: No, that's all right. Don't you worry about that. I'm a member of the Club and I can take you in the Members' Enclosure as my guests.

JENNINGS: Members' Enclosure! Oh, *thank* you, Mr. Findlater: won't that be super, Darbi?

DARBISHIRE: Simply smashing. Padded seats, too, I shouldn't wonder. All the rest of the chaps'll be in the cheap ones on the far side. They'll be queueing up to get *our* autographs when they know where we are.

Bring up engine, fade out.

Fade in cricket ball on bat, clapping applause, etc.

MR. WILKINS: Oh, well played, sir. Beautiful shot, wasn't it, Carter?

MR. CARTER: Yes, very nice stroke, and off the first ball he received, too. Did you see that, Venables and Atkinson? That's the way to make an off-drive.

VENABLES: Yes, sir: who's the batsman, sir?

MR. CARTER: That's R.J.Findlater: the one who's just come in.

TEMPLE: May I borrow your field glasses, sir? I want to get a close-up.

MR. CARTER: Here you are.

21

TEMPLE: Thank you, sir... I say, I can see wizardly now. I can even see the umpire's moustache.

ATKINSON: If that's all you want to look at, Temple, let me have the glasses. I want to see Findlater making another of those beefy off-drives.

TEMPLE: Wait a minute, Atkinson. I can see the grandstand now, and the Members' Enclosure.

Burst of clapping

MR. WILKINS: Oh, jolly good shot! Did you see that, you boys? Perfect boundary stroke. By jove, Findlater's in form this morning.

VENABLES: Jennings ought to be here, sir. He's as keen as socko on doing off-drives like that. He can do them jolly well, too.

MR. WILKINS: So I discovered in the classroom last night, and that's why he isn't here this morning.

TEMPLE: Oh, sir; Mr. Wilkins, sir; I believe Jennings *is* here.

MR. WILKINS: Eh? Don't be ridiculous, boy! You're imagining things. Must be looking through the wrong end of the glasses or something. Let me have a look... I can only see two elderly gentlemen in straw hats sitting next to... Good heavens! I say, Carter, the boy's right: it's Jennings and Darbishire. You have a look through the binoculars.

Reaction from boys

But... but... What are they doing here? They're supposed to be at school doing an English exercise – picking out objects and things.

MR. CARTER: Well, we seem to have picked out a couple of objects through the field glasses. You'd better go and investigate at once, before the lunch interval, while I look after the remainder.

MR. WILKINS: I certainly will: it's... it's... preposterous. I'm going straight over there this minute!

VENABLES: Oh, but, sir; you can't, sir!

MR. WILKINS: Oh! And why not?

VENABLES: They're in the enclosure, sir, and they won't let you in unless you're a member.

MR. WILKINS: I... I... corwumph!

Fade, fade in applause and clapping. Mr Willkins calling, distant:

Jennings and Darbishire, come here at once! (*approach*) What on earth are you boys doing in there? Come here immediately. Don't you know you're not allowed in the enclosure? It's

22

private – reserved for members only.

JENNINGS: (*approaching*) But we are sort of temporary members, sir. We were invited in by R.J.Findlater.

MR. WILKINS: Nonsense: he's out at the wicket. Why should he invite you in?

JENNINGS: Well, I just happened to mention that I'd played for the second eleven, and as one cricketer to another he brought us along, sir.

MR. WILKINS: Oh! Did he? And did you happen to mention "as one cricketer to another" that you were supposed to be at school doing some work for me?

JENNINGS: That was really why we came, sir. You said we'd got to bring the work to you as soon as we'd finished, and we didn't want to disappoint you, sir.

DARBISHIRE: Yes, before lunch you said, sir. So we've brought our books for you to correct.

MR. WILKINS: I... I...

JENNINGS: Gosh! And we're only just in time. Look, the teams are going in for lunch now. Phew! That was a near squeak: but we haven't let you down, sir. You'll find the exercises with our compliments and things, just as you told us.

Music, fade in cricket background

MR. CARTER: Well, come along, you boys: we're going back to school now. The Head wants us home by six o'clock.

VENABLES: Oh, sir, can't we stop till they draw stumps, sir?

MR. CARTER: I'm afraid not. I said we'd wait till the tea interval, and then we'd have to go. There won't be much more excitement now Findlater's out.

ATKINSON: Jolly wizard innings wasn't it, sir? A hundred and seventeen and most of them in off-drives.

MR. CARTER: Yes, very good stroke play, Atkinson. (*Going*) Come along then, everybody. Start making for the gate.

VENABLES: Let's be first in the bus, shall we, Atkinson? (*Going*) Then we'll be able to bag the front seats.

ATKINSON: (*going*) Righto! Come on!

MR. WILKINS: (*approach*) Hurry up you boys! Leave your places quietly and don't straggle. Come along, Darbishire: be quick, boy.

DARBISHIRE: Yes, sir... Oh, sir, I've just remembered – my autograph book, sir.

MR. WILKINS: What about it?

DARBISHIRE: It's in the Pavilion, sir. I gave it to Mr. Findlater to sign, and then you called us out of the enclosure, and I didn't see him to get it back.

MR. WILKINS: Can't help that now. You'll have to go without it.

DARBISHIRE: Oh, but, sir, I can't. It's practically invaluable. It's got all sorts of autographs - film stars, sporting characters, famous authors, cabinet ministers, and our window-cleaner's cousin, sir.

MR. WILKINS: What shall we do, Carter? Has he time to go and get it?

MR. CARTER: Oh, I suppose so. Hurry up then, Darbishire, and don't stay. Go straight out and join us by the gate.

DARBISHIRE: Thank you, sir.

JENNINGS: May I go with him, sir, and help him find it?

MR. CARTER: (*going*) Quickly then: we're late as it is.

JENNINGS: Come on, Darbi, let's run... You are a ruin not remembering it before. The teams are having tea in the Pavilion now. Mr. Findlater won't come out till he's finished, and they're not letting anyone in unless they've got their membership cards.

DARBISHIRE: Oh, gosh, what on earth shall I do, then? If he won't come out, and I can't go in, what about my book? I've only got a few minutes!

JENNINGS: Well, it's no good waiting about in front. I vote we slip round the back of the Pavilion and see if we can see them having tea. We might even possibly wave to Mr. Findlater through the window or something and get him to...

DARBISHIRE: All right: buck up, then. Let's go this way.

Fade out/in

JENNINGS: This is the place. The windows are a bit high: I can't see through. Give me a leg up, Darbi.

DARBISHIRE: Okay: (*heave*) gosh, you're heavy! I can't hold you much longer – oh! That's better. Well, can you see them having tea?

JENNINGS: No, this isn't the tea-room window: it's the changing room. I can see Mr. Findlater's cricket bag in the corner.

DARBISHIRE: What of it?

JENNINGS: Your autograph book may still be inside.

DARBISHIRE: · That doesn't help much: we're still outside!

JENNINGS: I know, but the window isn't fastened. All you've got to do is to nip in and grab your book.

DARBISHIRE: Who! Me? Gosh, no: I might get arrested.

JENNINGS: Don't be so feeble, Darbi: it's your own property.

DARBISHIRE: I know, but – well, the bag might be locked.

JENNINGS: It isn't: I've just told you, it's open.

DARBISHIRE: No, you said it was the window that was open.

JENNINGS: Don't talk such antiseptic eyewash. If you're afraid, I'll come with you.

DARBISHIRE: Oh, well, that's different. I'll go if you'll come.

JENNINGS: Right: give me a leg up a bit further. A bit more... That's it... Now I can open the window.

Window opens

Hurry up, Jen, Mr. Carter'll be getting restive.

JENNINGS: I'm in now. Give me your hand and I'll pull you up. Mind your shins... good work, you've made it. Now, there's the cricket bag in the corner by the door.

DARBISHIRE: Oh, wizzo! (*going*) Let's have a look... (*approach*) Yes, here's my book inside it. Let's go now, before anyone...

JENNINGS: (*whispering*) Ssh! Ssh! Darbi, listen!

DARBISHIRE: (*whispering*) What's the matter?

JENNINGS: There's someone in here. I caught sight of a man behind the cupboard, in that alcove at the other end of the room. It must be one of the cricketers.

DARBISHIRE: Oh, golly, what a bish! Well, why doesn't he come out and catch us then?

JENNINGS: I don't know. He must have heard us: perhaps he's changing his clothes.

DARBISHIRE: Well, we'll have to go and say something. We can't just fly in and out of the window like bluebottles, or he'll think it a bit queer.

JENNINGS: Okay. (*turn*) Come on then... (*normal*) Er... good afternoon.

MAN: (*low and furtive, shady character*) What do you want in here? Go away, can't you?

JENNINGS: I'm sorry if we disturbed you while you were changing. We just came in about the autographs.

DARBISHIRE: Yes: we thought all the players were having tea.

MAN: Yes, that's right – so they are. I've had my tea. Just

25

came in to change.

DARBISHIRE: I wonder if you'd mind giving me your autograph, now we've met. I'm trying to collect as many as I can. Look – there are six empty pink pages for sporting characters at the end.

MAN: Autograph? Eh! Oh! See what you mean. All right, give me the book. Let me see now... There you are. Now I've got to get moving.

DARBISHIRE: Thank you so much. I'm awfully... (*Door slam*) Oh! He's got moving already.

JENNINGS: Yes, and so had we better or we'll miss the bus. Come on: I'll get out of the window first.

DARBISHIRE: Hey! Stop half a mo, Jen.

JENNINGS: I can't – we've wasted enough half mo's as it is.

DARBISHIRE: Yes, but look here, this doesn't make sense. That chap doesn't know his own name. Look what he's signed in my book – R.J.Findlater!

JENNINGS: That's crazy: that wasn't Findlater. Dash it all, he's the one chap we *do* know he wasn't!

DARBISHIRE: Perhaps he's a forger.

JENNINGS: Don't be so bats. There's no point in forging your signature in an autograph book. Now if it was a cheque it would be different.

DARBISHIRE: What would be different – the signature?

JENNINGS: No, you goof! I expect that chap was just pulling your leg. Ha, ha, ha! I bet he's laughing like a couple of drains. He's probably telling Mr. Findlater that he's signed his name for him.

DARBISHIRE: It's not fair, forging autograph books. I'll have to rub it all out now, and besides, the proper Mr. Findlater hasn't signed it yet. These pages are still all pink, except this one.

JENNINGS: Well, you've had it now, Darbi. You've got your book back, that's something. Come on. I'll climb down out of the window first, and when...

Door opens

FINDLATER: (*approach*) Hullo, hullo... Now what on earth are you two boys doing in the players' dressing-room?

JENNINGS: Oh, gosh – it's Mr. Findlater, the real one this time. Congratulations on your century, sir.

FINDLATER: Thank you: but you shouldn't be in here, you know.

26

JENNINGS: We came in to get the autograph book: we couldn't get in the front way.

FINDLATER: Oh, yes, the book: I forgot to sign it, didn't I? I'll do it now.

DARBISHIRE: It's been done already by someone else. There was a man here when we came in, and he signed your name for me.

FINDLATER: Really! Let me see... h'mph... Someone's been playing a joke on you. Just a minute: I'll get my fountain pen and give you the real autograph... That's funny: I know I left my pen in my pocket... By jove! my wallet's gone too! What's been going on in here? Great heavens! Yes – and my watch has disappeared as well.

DARBISHIRE: Gosh!

JENNINGS: Wait a minute: I've got it!

FINDLATER: What, my watch?

JENNINGS: No, but I see what's happened. That chap who signed the book! I expect he's been round everyone else's jackets, too. He looked rather a shady character, didn't he, Darbi?

DARBISHIRE: Yes, he didn't look at all like a cricketer at all to me.

FINDLATER: (going) We'll soon see. (ad lib searching coats, then approach) Yes, you're right. The wallets have disappeared out of all these jackets. I expect their other valuables have gone, too.

DARBISHIRE: He had a bag with him: I thought it was his cricket gear.

JENNINGS: He can't have gone far. Shall we see if we can spot him outside?

FINDLATER: Yes: I'll come with you. He's probably making for the gates. (going) Come along – through here and down the Pavilion steps.

Bring up crowd background

You'll know him again if you see him?

JENNINGS: Oh, yes, easily.

DARBISHIRE: But, Jennings, what about Mr. Carter and Mr. Wilkins? They'll be hopping mad if we're away any longer.

JENNINGS: They'll have to hop then. This is more important. We'll probably run into them at the main gate, anyway.

DARBISHIRE: All right; you look out for the thief, and I'll look out for Mr. Wilkins. That's just as important as far as we're concerned.

FINDLATER: Give me the word at once if you spot him.

JENNINGS: Yes, righto. Gosh, the crowd's thick! We're going to have a job to pick him out.

DARBISHIRE: There he is: look! Over there by the gate. Oh, wizzo!

FINDLATER: Where?

DARBISHIRE: That man in the grey suit.

FINDLATER: I see him. (*going*) All right, leave this to me.

JENNINGS: Well, I can't see him, Darbi.

DARBISHIRE: Yes, over there where Mr. Findlater's going. He looks a bit fed up, too. After all, we've kept him waiting about ten minutes.

JENNINGS: Who're you talking about?

DARBISHIRE: Mr. Wilkins, of course.

JENNINGS: What! You great crumbling ruin, Darbishire – he's not the thief.

DARBISHIRE: I never said he was: *you're* supposed to be looking for the thief. *I* said I'd look for Mr. Wilkins and Mr. Carter.

JENNINGS: Oh gosh: we'd better go and rescue him. Mr. Findlater'll have him behind prison bars before he knows what's happening.

DARBISHIRE: Sorry: I got a bit mixed up. I should have explained to Mr. Findlater that it was really two men we were looking for – one tall and short, the other fat and thin – I mean...

JENNINGS: You're still a bit mixed up if you ask me.

DARBISHIRE: Yes, but what I meant was – Oh, I say, Jennings, quick: stop! There's the man we're after – over there, with the bag, look! He's making for the gates.

JENNINGS: Gosh, yes, we've got him now.

DARBISHIRE: We wizard well haven't. We've lost Mr. Findlater – he's chasing Mr. Wilkins.

JENNINGS: What a ghastly bish – look, you run after Mr. Findlater while I stop the thief.

DARBISHIRE: But how're you going to do it?

JENNINGS: Give me your autograph book.

DARBISHIRE: But I've got his autograph already, and it's no good anyway, because he isn't a sporting character.

JENNINGS: I know, but it'll be something to keep him talking, so he doesn't suspect. I'll ask him to write a bit more in it. (*going*) Hurry up: I shan't be able to hold him for long...

Cross fade to Mr. Wilkins

MR. WILKINS: My dear chap, I don't know what you're talking about. My name's Wilkins: I'm a master at Linbury Court School. I have *not* been in the Pavilion. I'm just waiting for a couple of boys to come out.

FINDLATER: So you admit you know they were in there?

MR. WILKINS: Of course they were in there: I said they could go. Some trumpery moonshine about an autograph book.

FINDLATER: They've identified you as the man who was in the changing room, and after you left, everybody's wallets were missing.

MR. WILKINS: But I... I...

FINDLATER: I shall have to ask you to accompany me to the Pavilion.

MR. WILKINS: But... but... this is preposterous! You must be out of your mind! I... I... corwumph!

DARBISHIRE: (*approaching*) Mr. Findlater! Oh, please, Mr. Findlater, you've got the wrong man. That's one of our masters. You see, I made a mistake.

FINDLATER: Mistake? Surely you know the difference between one of your own masters and a shady character, don't you?

DARBISHIRE: Well, yes; but listen – we've found the real thief now. He's over there: look! Jennings is trying to stop him.

FINDLATER: Righto, I'll come and cope. You'd better come along too – sorry, Mr. Wilkins.

(*Exit Findlater and Darbishire ad lib*)

MR. WILKINS: Yes, but what's happening? Dash it all, I...

MR. CARTER: (*approaching*) I say, what's going on, Wilkins? Haven't you found those boys yet? We're ten minutes late already.

MR. WILKINS: It's no good asking me what's going on, Carter. Everyone's going off, as far as I can see.

MR. CARTER: Going off where?

MR. WILKINS: Going off their heads. I've just been accused of burglary, and Darbishire and R.J.Findlater are dashing in and out of the crowd like grasshoppers. I don't know what it's all about.

MR. CARTER: We'd better go and see. We'll have to force our way through... Excuse me, please: excuse me, may I come past?

Murmurs from crowd

MR. WILKINS: What's happening, Carter, can you see?

MR. CARTER: Yes, Findlater's holding a man with a bag. There's a policeman coming up now to take charge. I think he's taking him away.

MR. WILKINS: And what about Jennings and Darbishire?

MR. CARTER: They're there too: they *would* be! Trust Jennings to get himself mixed up in a commotion. Oh, it's all right – I think they're coming now. (*Calling*) Jennings!... Darbishire!

JENNINGS: (*approaching*) Oh, there you are, sir. Oh, good. I'm sorry we're a bit late turning up. There's been a terrific hoo-hah. We've been helping Mr. Findlater, but it's all over now.

FINDLATER: (*approaching*) Yes, I'm afraid it's my fault they're late. If these boys hadn't been on the scene, both teams would have gone home with empty pockets this evening. I owe your colleague here an apology, I'm afraid. Darbishire told me he was the criminal.

MR. WILKINS: I... I... well... I...

DARBISHIRE: I'm terribly sorry, sir.

MR. CARTER: Come along, then.

JENNINGS: Yes, sir. Oh, Mr. Findlater, would you please sign Darbishire's book before we go? He wanted the autographs of both teams, but all he's got is a forgery.

FINDLATER: I'll go one better than that. The bat I used for my knock this afternoon was a new one. I'll get both teams to sign their names on it, and then I'll send it on to you. After all, they owe you something for saving their belongings.

JENNINGS: Oh, *thank* you, Mr. Findlater.

DARBISHIRE: Thank you very *much* Mr. Findlater.

JENNINGS: Thank you very much *indeed*, Mr. Findlater.

MR. CARTER: And now we'd better be getting back to school.

Fade out/music/fade in. Door knock

MR. WILKINS: Come in.

Door opens

JENNINGS: (*approach*) Oh, sir; Mr. Wilkins, sir.

MR. WILKINS: Oh, it's you, Jennings, is it? What do you want?

JENNINGS: Well, sir, you know you confiscated my old cricket bat the other day because I was using it indoors, sir?

MR. WILKINS: And oiling it all over the corridor – yes?

JENNINGS: Well, sir, do you think I could have it back, please? I want to practice off-drives – out of doors, this time, sir.

MR. WILKINS: Oh, do you? But why come and ask me for your old bat. You've got a new one now, signed by both the county teams.

JENNINGS: Yes, I know, sir, that's the trouble. You see, Darbishire didn't get his autographs the other afternoon, so we agreed that *he* should have the signatures and *I* should have the bat, sir.

MR. WILKINS: Sounds fair enough to me.

JENNINGS: But there's a ghastly snag that's cropped up, sir. They've signed their names all down the front, and now Darbishire says I mustn't let a hard object like a cricket ball hit my bat, because it'll ruin his autographs. He won't even let me oil it, sir!

MR.WILKINS: I see: very awkward. In that case I suppose I'd better give you your old one back. There you are.

JENNINGS: Thank you, sir.

MR. WILKINS: But don't run away with the idea, Jennings, that because you can't use your new bat on a hard cricket ball, you can use your *old* one on a soft blackboard duster; or you'll find that no amount of bat oil will calm the troubled waters that will be breaking over your head. Eh? What? What? (*Breaks into Wilkins' curtain laughter*)

Fade out. Music.

Linbury Court Preparatory School

Dear David,

Up to now Darbishire and I have only collected engine numbers, but as stamps are better we have taken up philately latterly. But I must warn you there are snags that you don't know about. And if you are like me and only have a small income you will surprised at the outcome as we were when we accidentally did a scientific chemical test in the gutter-spout. I have now got most stamps, except an unused 2½d English one for your envelope, which is why you will have to pay extra when you get this letter, but perhaps you won't mind.

Must stop now, owing to no blotch, but will tell you all about it on Wed.

Yours affeckly,

J.C.T. Jennings.

JENNINGS
AND THE PENNY BLACK

(Fourth series no.2)

Jennings and the Penny Black was the
twenty-second Jennings play.

It was first broadcast by the BBC Home Service for Children's Hour
on Wednesday 7th November 1951, with the following cast:

JENNINGS	John Charlesworth
DARBISHIRE	Henry Searle
VENABLES	Bill Croydon
TEMPLE	Lance Secretan
ATKINSON	Malcolm Hillier
MR. CARTER	Geoffrey Wincott
MR. WILKINS	Wilfred Babbage

Produced by David Davis

Fade in dormitory rising bell

ATKINSON: Wake up, Darbishire, wake up.

DARBISHIRE: What's that? Is it time to get up already?

VENABLES: Of course it is: the bell went hours ago.

DARBISHIRE: It always is time for something before you're ready for it. (*Yawns*) You know, Venables, it seems only yesterday that I went to bed.

VENABLES: Well, so it was. You wouldn't say crazy things like that if you were awake. Go on, Darbi, get up! I'll race you getting dressed.

DARBISHIRE: I don't think I'll bother to race. I like to come to gradually and practise my knots.

VENABLES: What knots?

DARBISHIRE: You mean which knots – not whatnots. Whatnots are something quite different.

VENABLES: Different from what?

DARBISHIRE: (*yawns*) I don't know: different from which knots, I suppose. What I mean is, I always like to tie a couple of clove hitches in my dressing-gown cord before I get out of bed. It's useful too. People often tie knots in things to remind them not to forget things.

VENABLES: What have you specially got to remember?

DARBISHIRE: Well, tying knots in my dressing-gown cord reminds me I've got to get up as soon as I've done it.

ATKINSON: You're just lazy, Darbishire. Look at Jennings: he's practically dressed already.

DARBISHIRE: Goodness! So he is! What's the rush, Jen? I bet you haven't washed.

JENNINGS: I wizard well have, Darbishire. Well, I've had a series of lightning rinses. I don't see much point in washing too hard – you only get dirty again in an hour or two.

DARBISHIRE: Yes, there's something in that, Jennings. On the other hand, why bother to eat breakfast? You'll only be hungry again in an hour or two. What's the hurry, anyway?

JENNINGS: Surely you haven't forgotten, Darbi? We arranged to get downstairs before the postman comes. We don't want to miss him this morning.

DARBISHIRE: Golly, yes, of course, I'd forgotten. I must get dressed in top gear. Today's the day, isn't it?

JENNINGS: It certainly is. I'm surprised at you sitting there tying

34

clove hitches in your dressing gown cord while the postman's struggling up the drive with our sheet.

VENABLES: With your what, Jennings?

JENNINGS: Our sheet. Darbi and I sent for one on approval.

ATKINSON: Whatever did you want to do that for?

DARBISHIRE: To see if we approve of it, of course, Atki. They send loose ones, you know.

VENABLES: Obviously; you couldn't send them through the post if they were tucked in. But why sheets? Why not blankets or eiderdowns?

JENNINGS: Oh, it isn't that sort of sheet: ours are foreign stamps. Darbi and I are starting a collection. And they're free, too. Look, I'll show you the advertisement. I cut it out of the magazine when I wrote for them. Here it is.

VENABLES: (*reading*) "Free on appro, 50 rare foreign stamps given away with each sheet of genuine Colonial and Empire issues. Send for free lists and sheets on approval. No obligation. S&S Boddington Limited, Philitalasts – er – Philastilists... Philistinists..."

DARBISHIRE: Philatelists! That means stamp collectors.

JENNINGS: Yes, isn't it super – absolutely free! And you don't even have to be obliged if you don't want to. Mind you we're not going to be ungrateful. We shall be obliged as two coots if they give us that lot for nothing.

VENABLES: Surely there's something to pay?

JENNINGS: No, there isn't. I think they do it for advertisement. There's nothing about sending any dosh. We shouldn't have written otherwise, because Darbi and I are both broke as a reed.

ATKINSON: I say, what a decent firm S&S Boddington must be! Fancy giving them away.

DARBISHIRE: Yes, you don't often find firms who are philanthropists, do you?

VENABLES: If they deal in stamps they must be.

DARBISHIRE: Oh, no, not nesser-celery. A philanthropist is a chap who gives money and stuff away.

VENABLES: You've just said it was a chap who collects stamps.

DARBISHIRE: No, that was a philatelist. You're getting muddled up because they both start with phil. My father says phil is one of those Greek prefixes: it means loving and...

ATKINSON: You mean prefects. Only an ignorant coot would call them prefixes. Not that any of ours are all that loving.

VENABLES: I should think they jolly well aren't. We could do with a few more prefects like Phil at this school.

DARBISHIRE: You don't understand, you thick boneheads. A philatelist is a lover of stamps – and a philanthropist loves giving things away.

JENNINGS: Well, that proves S&S Boddington must be both. They're dishing them out for nothing so fast they'll have to start collecting again soon or they won't have any left.

ATKINSON: (off) Here's the postman coming up the drive now.

JENNINGS: Oh, wizzo, let's go and meet him, Darbi.

DARBISHIRE: I'm not dressed yet.

JENNINGS: Well, I'm jolly well not going to wait for you. It's too bad, Darbishire. I've been ready for ages and I'll miss him if I don't go now. Cheerio, see you later.

DARBISHIRE: Oh, Jennings, come back!

JENNINGS: What's the matter?

DARBISHIRE: You'll have to get dressed all over again. You've forgotten to put your vest on. Here it is, on the floor.

JENNINGS: Oh, fish-hooks! What a swizz! Now, we'll have to wait till Mr. Carter gives the post out after breakfast.

DARBISHIRE: You were in too much of a hurry, getting a move on. My father says – "More haste less speed" is a proverb which people would do well to...

Fade out/music/dining-room b/g

TEMPLE: Sir, is there a letter for me, sir?

MR. CARTER: Yes, here you are, Temple.

TEMPLE: Thank you, sir.

ATKINSON: What about me, sir?

MR. CARTER: Nothing for you, Atkinson. Sorry. There's one for Jennings, though.

JENNINGS: Oh, good, sir. Do you hear that Darbi – it's come.

MR. CARTER: Here you are.

JENNINGS: Thank you, sir. It's jolly important, this letter. It's from a firm of philanthropologists, sir.

MR. CARTER: Really!

JENNINGS: Come on, Darbi, let's open it... Don't crowd round you chaps. Budge out of the light, Venables, I can't see.

Buzz of conversation, envelope opened

There you are. What do you think of that?

DARBISHIRE: How wizard! A whole sheet of Colonial and Empire stamps!

JENNINGS: Yes, and these fifty rare ones, obligingly thrown in, without obligation, don't forget: and all for nothing! I say, these Boddington characters must be a decent couple of chaps. I hardly like to take all these.

VENABLES: I'll take some, if you don't want them.

TEMPLE: Yes, so will I.

JENNINGS: What d'you think, Darbi? Shall we give some away?

DARBISHIRE: Oh, I think we should. After all, Messrs. Boddington have been wizardly generous to us, so it's only fair we should be the same. My father says: "Do unto others..."

JENNINGS: Righto then, let's share them out. We can easily get some more if we write for them.

ATKINSON: Coo, thanks Jennings. Can I have this Nigerian one? Oh, yes, and this Barbados as well?

JENNINGS: Help yourself, Atki.

TEMPLE: Have you got any old English ones, Jennings? I'm collecting anything from Queen Victoria onwards.

VENABLES: I'd rather have some of these loose ones. Look, what about these, Jennings?

JENNINGS: Wait a minute: don't grab – there's plenty for everyone. You can have these, Venables.

VENABLES: Coo, thanks, Jen.

ATKINSON: I say, Bromwich Major'd like this one: he goes in for Australians.

TEMPLE: Yes, and here's quite a rare South African. I should give that to Binns Minor, Jennings, because his uncle nearly went there once.

JENNINGS: Right: look, Venables, I've given you yours: go and tell anyone in Form 3 that if they'd like to come along now, without obligation, Darbi and I are giving stamps away.

Fade out/fade in

Well, now everybody's got some. H'm! We don't seem to have got many left for ourselves, do we Darbi?

DARBISHIRE: Never mind, Jennings, I've got quite a warm glow inside me from bringing so much happiness to other people. That's how you feel when you go in for philanthropy in a big way.

JENNINGS: What about S&S Boddington, then? They must be

glowing like a couple of blast furnaces with all the free sheets they dish out. Let's see what we've got left. H'm! There's no more left of the Colonial and Empires, but there's a few odd ones in the free packet. Here's a red 2 cent U.S.A. Pity – I've got that already.

DARBISHIRE: Yes, and here's another – and another; and oh, gosh! Jen, that's all we've got left.

JENNINGS: It strikes me, Darbi, we've been a wizard sight too generous.   Gosh, what ozzard swizzlers Venables and Temple and Co. are! They've got the pick of the bunch, without obligation, and only left us these rotten ones. I vote we write for some more, and keep them for ourselves this time.

DARBISHIRE: You don't think the Boddingtons will think we're being greedy, do you?

JENNINGS: Oh, no! It'll give them a chance to glow a bit more. Here's Mr. Carter. I must tell him... sir, have you heard about our stamps?

MR. CARTER: (*approaching*) I certainly have, Jennings. Everywhere I go I meet boys clutching handfuls of stamps which they tell me you've been giving away. Is that right?

JENNINGS: Yes, sir. Darbishire and I are feeling rather philatelic this morning, sir.

MR. CARTER: It's quite all right, of course, but it seems more than generous to give away your whole collection.

JENNINGS: That's all right, sir. They were just a few stamps we were given for nothing.

MR. CARTER: Are you sure it's for nothing, Jennings?

JENNINGS: Yes, sir; here's the advertisement, sir.   Look – absolutely free and there's nothing about having to pay for them.

MR. CARTER: They say that to encourage you to write for them. Look at it again: "50 rare foreign stamps given away with each sheet of our..." H'm! That means you get the ones in the packet free, but you've got to pay for the stamps on the sheet.

JENNINGS: } What?

DARBISHIRE: } *Pay* for them, sir!

JENNINGS: Oh, what a rotten swizz, sir!

MR. CARTER: It's quite a common practice.   Now where is this sheet?

JENNINGS: Here, sir, only there are no stamps left now. And – oh, goodness! I never spotted that before. Look, Darbi, down at the bottom. It's got the price of each one. Twelve Colonials at twopence and... heavens, the whole sheet's worth five shillings.

DARBISHIRE: Phew! What a ghastly catastroscope.

MR. CARTER: You'll either have to send the money or return the stamps to them.

JENNINGS: But, sir, we haven't got any money.

MR. CARTER: You'd better get the stamps back, then.

JENNINGS: Yes, that's what we'll do, sir. We'll tell everyone we've made a bit of a bish and want them back, and I'll post them off tomorrow.

DARBISHIRE: But what an ozzard swizzle; there we were, glowing with the joy of giving and thinking S&S Boddington were, too.

JENNINGS: Strikes me we've been hornswoggled under false pretences. If I ever meet S&S Boddington, Esquire, I shall tell him straight out...

MR. CARTER: The first thing to do, Jennings, is to try and retrieve as many of those stamps as you can: and that may not be too easy.

Fade out/fade in

JENNINGS: Oh, there you are, Atkinson: listen, I'm terribly sorry but there's been a bit of a bish. You'll have to give those stamps I gave you this morning back again.

ATKINSON: But I haven't got them any more, Jennings. I swapped them with Bromwich Major for a busted penknife.

JENNINGS: Tut! I'd better go and see Bromwich, then.

ATKINSON: He hasn't got them now, either. He swapped them with Rumbelow for a tennis ball. And I happen to know Rumbelow was hoping to pass them on to Martin-Jones for a hunk of milk chocolate.

JENNINGS: This is hopeless: they may have gone half round the school by this time.

ATKINSON: Super sorrow: but you did say we could keep them. I tell you what, though – I'll give you the penknife Bromwich gave me, if he'll give me the tennis ball he got from Rumbelow.

JENNINGS: Yes, but that'll mean he'll want Martin-Jones's hunk of milk chocolate to make up, and I expect he's eaten it now, and... Oh, here you are, Darbishire – any luck?

DARBISHIRE: (*approaching*) No: I can't get on the track of them at all. I've been trying half the afternoon, but Brown Major's swapped his stamps for an old torch battery, and goodness knows where they've got to now. He says we can have the battery, though, if the chap he's swapped the stamps with will...

JENNINGS: All right, all right, I've just been through all that with Atkinson, and it's no good anyway. What would S&S Boddington think if we sent them busted penknives and old batteries! We've either got to send their stamps back, or the five shillings to pay for them. They'll be setting solicitors and bloodhounds and things after us, if they think we're trying to swizzle them.

DARBISHIRE: But we aren't! They swizzled us. Why couldn't they say in the first place... Oh, this is hopeless: what shall we do?

JENNINGS: We'll have to press on with the search and get those stamps by hook or by crook, or by tomorrow morning at the latest.

DARBISHIRE: Look, there's Venables: we haven't asked him.

JENNINGS: (*calling*) Venables...! I say, Venables, you know those stamps we gave you this morning?

VENABLES: What about them?

JENNINGS: There's been a bish: they've got to go back. Have you still got the ones we gave you?

VENABLES: Yes.

JENNINGS: Oh, good. Can we have them, then?

VENABLES: Yes, they're over there in my locker. You can get them yourself, can't you? I'm just going to put my name down for the ping-pong tournament.

JENNINGS: Oh, thanks.

VENABLES: You'll find them next to my paint box. I was doing some painting after lunch, and I thought...

JENNINGS: Okay, we'll find them. Come on, Darbi... Here we are – here's his locker. (*Locker opens*) And here are the stamps, all unswapped next to his paint box, just as he said.

DARBISHIRE: But, Jen, these are no good: these are out of the free packet that we could keep anyway.

JENNINGS: Looks like it, doesn't it: just the usual 2 cent American ones and a few old Queen Victorias, and – I say,

Darbi, look at this!

DARBISHIRE: What?

JENNINGS: This stamp, here: golly, it's a Queen Victoria Penny Black – well, what do you know!

DARBISHIRE: Penny Black? Gosh, that's one of the rarest stamps you can have. They were the first ones to be issued. Are you sure?

JENNINGS: Of course I'm sure! Head of Queen Victoria – one penny – and it's black all right. It's as black as your handkerchief. I say, I bet S&S Boddington don't know they've let a priceless stamp like this get in to their free packet by mistake. It's worth – well, I don't know – pounds, perhaps.

DARBISHIRE: How super-socko-sonic! But it's not really ours, is it? We gave it to Venables.

JENNINGS: Ah, but we didn't know it was priceless, then. And anyway he said we could have it back. Look, Darbi, this is going to make everything come out all right. We can see the penny black for, well – say about £25, or whatever it's worth: then we can send the Boddingtons their five shillings, and perhaps even give Venables something, for being so decent about giving it back.

DARBISHIRE: Yes, we could go fifty-fifty with him: fifty for you, fifty for me and – er – Venables can have what's left.

JENNINGS: First of all, we'll have to find someone to buy it.

DARBISHIRE: Temple's got a decent stamp collection. And I happen to know he collects ancient Britain's too.

JENNINGS: Ancient Britains! This is only Queen Victoria, it's not Boadicea.

DARBISHIRE: Well, early British, I should say. Let's ask him if he'll buy it.

JENNINGS: What, for £25! Don't be crazy! I doubt if he's got more than five shillings.

DARBISHIRE: Well, that'd do for the Boddington's postal order; and if he's willing to fork out any more, well, that'll be sheer profit, won't it? We could treat Venables to a smashing seven course high tea at Mrs. Lumley's café in the village.

JENNINGS: Yes, we could have ice-cream, doughnuts, baked beans, fizzy ginger pop, spaghetti on toast, cream buns – that's six courses: what else?

DARBISHIRE: I've got a home-made cake in my tuck box: we could give him a hunk of that.

JENNINGS: That's fine then – that's the seven courses exactly.

41

DARBISHIRE: On the other hand, we've had all the worry and headache: I don't think we need go to ginger pop *and* ice cream just for Venables.

JENNINGS: All right – let's wipe those out. And I don't think he likes baked beans much, either.

DARBISHIRE: And I don't like spaghetti, so we'll have to rule those out, too.

JENNINGS: Righto, that still leaves – you know, Darbi, the last time I had doughnuts and cream buns at Mrs. Lumley's, I didn't feel too well after it. I think it would be better just to give Venables a slice of your home-made cake and leave out the rest.

DARBISHIRE: Perhaps you're right. We could be terribly decent to him for a few days to make up for his missing the other six courses... There he is going back: (*calling*) I say, Venables, we've got the stamps out of your locker. Thanks for being so decent. Would you like a piece of home-made cake?

VENABLES: Yes, I would, thanks very much.

DARBISHIRE: Come with me then, and I'll...

JENNINGS: No, not *now*, Darbi, you prehistoric remains – *afterwards*. We've got to fix things up with Temple first.

DARBISHIRE: Oh, yes, of course. Have you seen Temple anywhere, Venables?

VENABLES: Yes, he's outside on the quad.

JENNINGS: Come on then, Darbi.

VENABLES: Hey, what about my cake?

DARBISHIRE: (*off*) Well, it depends what Temple says. Come and see me later. I may be able to give it to you then.

JENNINGS: Come on, Darbi, quick – don't waste time.

DARBISHIRE: No, of course not. I hope we can persuade him to buy it. We mustn't try and force it on him, though. My father says: "Persuasion is..."

Fade out/fade in

JENNINGS: There's Temple over there, playing football with Bromwich Major. (*calling*) Hey, Temple! Here a minute. We've got something for you.

TEMPLE: (*approaching*) What is it?

JENNINGS: Look, would you be willing to give anything from five shillings upwards for a penny stamp? – It's been used.

TEMPLE: You must be bats: I can get an unused one for a penny.

DARBISHIRE: Ah, but this isn't an ordinary penny stamp. It's a genuine eighteen forty-something Queen Victoria penny black – one of the first stamps ever issued.

TEMPLE: You haven't got a penny black!

JENNINGS: We jolly well have! It was in the free packet. We didn't even have to pay a penny for it.

TEMPLE: Goodness, you are lucky! If it's a good one, it'll be worth – well, say, perhaps for instance, about £25. I'll give you five shillings for it for my collection. Where is it?

DARBISHIRE: It's here, in my trouser pocket.

TEMPLE: In your...! Gosh, Darbishire, you must be stark raving crackers! You don't carry rare stamps about, all rolled up with handkerchiefs, toffee papers and things. You mustn't even hold it with your fingers: you're supposed to use tweezers.

DARBISHIRE: Oh, sorry: I didn't know. You see, we've only become interested in philately latterly.

TEMPLE: You've only done what?

DARBISHIRE: Collected stamps lately. Here it is, look!

JENNINGS: Take your great talons off it, Darbishire. You'll ruin it. You heard what Temple said: lay it in the palm of your hand.

TEMPLE: Let me see: yes, it's a Queen Victoria all right, and it's black, too. Righto, let's go indoors out of this wind and I'll ask Mr. Carter for five shillings from my bank.

JENNINGS: You're getting a bargain, don't forget. You said yourself it was worth about...

DARBISHIRE: Oh, help, help! Oh, I say, it's blown away!

TEMPLE: What?

JENNINGS: Look, there it is, blowing across the quad.

TEMPLE: After it – quick! Come on.

Running footsteps

JENNINGS: You are a great clumsy bazooka, Darbishire. Why didn't you hold it tight?

DARBISHIRE: You told me not to. You said lay it on the palm of my hand and use tweezers.

JENNINGS: Come on – faster; it's swirling about like blinko. Oh, gosh, it's gone.

TEMPLE: No, it hasn't: there it is, blowing towards the steps.

JENNINGS: We'll never catch it in this wind - not without tweezers.

DARBISHIRE: I tell you what: I'll go and fetch my butterfly net and we can stalk it with that.

JENNINGS: Buck up then, Darbi, or it'll be too late. Get some tweezers, too... Come on, Temple, we mustn't let it get away. There it goes. Goodness, it's sailing right up out of reach.

TEMPLE: We must get it, somehow. Oh, heavens, it's blowing up on to the roof.

JENNINGS: I can still see it. It's crash landed in the gutter: right over that upstairs window. If we go up there and climb on to the window sill, we should be able to reach it.

TEMPLE: Come on then – which room is it?

JENNINGS: It's... Oh, gosh, of course, it's Mr. Wilkins' room. He won't let us hop in and out on his window ledge, not even for a five shilling stamp.

TEMPLE: It's not a five shilling stamp – it's a penny one.

JENNINGS: Well, in that case you owe me four and eleven pence change, or rather... Well, never mind that now. I'll go and ask Old Wilkie if I can kindly do rescue operations from his room. You stay here on the quad in case it blows down; and when Darbishire gets back... Oh, here he is! Come on, Darbi, you and I have got to beetle up to Wilkie's room in top gear: come this way, it's quicker... I expect the gutter will be full of water after that rain this morning and...

DARBISHIRE: Phew! Not so fast. I've been running. I've got my butterfly net, you see. Matron wouldn't let me have any tweezers to pick it up with, so I had a bit of a brainwave and borrowed this pair of pliers from the carpenter's shop. They're a bit clumsy, of course, but...

Fade out/in

JENNINGS: Here we are: bags you knock.

DARBISHIRE: No, bags you. After all I'm carrying the tools.

JENNINGS: Righto, then.

(Door knocks repeated)

No answer. He must be out.

DARBISHIRE: Oh, fishhooks: what a bind!

JENNINGS: It isn't: it's a jolly wizard streak of luck. If he was in, he mightn't let us get cracking on the salvage work, but if the room's empty – well, it won't take a sec to nip inside, stand on his window sill and reach up to the gutter.

DARBISHIRE: It's a bit risky. You know what Old Wilkie's like, and my father says: "It's better to be safe..."

JENNINGS: Oh, come on, Darbi: I'm not going to lose a priceless, invaluable penny stamp, worth anything from five shillings to twenty five pounds: besides, think of S&S Boddington. If we don't get that stamp back, Temple won't give us the money to send them.

DARBISHIRE: All right then.

Door opens

JENNINGS: Come on: there's no one here. I'll nip on to the window sill and you hold me... That's right... Tut! I can't quite reach the gutter. Pass me the net.

DARBISHIRE: Be careful you don't fall. You don't want to pancake, slap-bang-doyng on to the quad... Oh, golly, Jen, there's someone coming along the corridor!

JENNINGS: Shut the door, quick, then they won't see us. (*Door shuts*) We'll be safe enough now. I don't suppose Mr. Wilkins'll be back just yet.

DARBISHIRE: Now where did I put the net? I know, I left it handy, so I could...

Door opens

MR. WILKINS: (*approaching*) I... I... corwumph! What on earth are you boys doing in here?

JENNINGS: Oh, sir, Mr. Wilkins, sir...

MR. WILKINS: Come down from that window sill at once, Jennings! What do you mean by marching into my room, without permission, and slamming the door in my face as soon as my back's turned?

JENNINGS: Sorry, sir: we did knock, but there was no answer, so we came in to – er – to make sure you were out, sir.

MR. WILKINS: You should have waited outside, if you wanted to see me. And what's all this clutter on my armchair?

DARBISHIRE: Oh, that's my butterfly net, sir. I'll move it.

MR. WILKINS: But why bring it into my room? You don't expect to catch butterflies on my bookshelf in the middle of November, do you?

DARBISHIRE: No, sir.

MR. WILKINS: And what are you doing on the window sill, Jennings? Listening for the cuckoo, I suppose?

JENNINGS: No, sir, we came in to ask you if we could get a stamp, sir.

MR. WILKINS: I don't reckon to give stamps out at this time of the afternoon. After chapel on Sunday is the proper time.

JENNINGS: I know, sir, but this is different: it's something urgent we've got to...

MR. WILKINS: Well, if it's urgent, bring the letter to me and I'll stamp it and take the money off your bank on Sunday.

JENNINGS: Oh, but sir, we don't want to post a letter, sir – at least not yet.

MR. WILKINS: Well, what on earth do you want me to sell you a stamp for?

JENNINGS: We don't, sir.

MR. WILKINS: But, you silly little boy, you just said you did! What is all this trumpery moonshine about? If you want a letter stamped, you can bring it to me.

JENNINGS: But it isn't an ordinary English stamp we want, sir.

MR. WILKINS: What is it then – a foreign one?

DARBISHIRE: No, it isn't a foreign one, sir – it's an English one. At least...

MR. WILKINS: You'd better go away and make up your mind what you *do* want. And take this butterfly net and these pliers with you, Darbishire. I can't think why you had to bring them here, anyway.

DARBISHIRE: Well, sir, if we'd got the stamp, I was going to use them to pick it up with, sir.

MR. WILKINS: Pick it up with pliers! It's not infectious, is it?

DARBISHIRE: Oh no, sir.

MR. WILKINS: Never heard such nonsense. You'll be telling me next that you need the butterfly net to catch it with.

DARBISHIRE: Yes, that's right, sir; that's what we were hoping to do; in case it got away again you see...

MR. WILKINS: I... I... corwumph! I...

JENNINGS: Come on, Darbishire, we won't bother Mr. Wilkins any longer.

Door shuts

DARBISHIRE: Well, that's bished things up nicely, I must say. What are we going to do now?

JENNINGS: I vote we try and get it from the classroom: it's next door to Wilkie's room, and if I lean out of the window I might be able to reach along the gutter and hoik it out.

DARBISHIRE: Yes, wizard wheeze! Come on: we mustn't waste time or it'll float away. Gosh, these stamps have caused us a lot of trouble, haven't they? Mind you, I know you shouldn't look gift horses in the mouth, but if I'd known of the hoo-hah it was going to lead to, I'd have said S&S Boddington could keep them and welcome.

JENNINGS: I agree: their gift stamps are bad enough: we don't want them giving us horses as well.

DARBISHIRE: No, you idiot, there aren't any horses really. It's just a saying. For instance, if we'd had a gift of horses from S&S Boddington, and we'd looked them in the mouth, we could have told how old they were.

JENNINGS: Who, S&S Boddington?

DARBISHIRE: No, you prehistoric remains – the horses.

JENNINGS: But you just said there weren't any horses. Strikes me you're getting a bit feeble-minded, Darbi. You're rambling like a couple of coots.

DARBISHIRE: Yes, but...

TEMPLE: (*approaching*) Oh, there you are, Jennings: have you got it yet?

JENNINGS: Hello, Temple. No, we're still on the trail.

TEMPLE: Well, you'd better buck up. It's not doing a valuable penny stamp any good lying face downwards in a gutter full of water – it's probably worth only half its value now.

DARBISHIRE: It couldn't be: there's no such thing as a halfpenny black.

JENNINGS: Here we are! I'll get on the window sill. (*Window opens*) Oh heavens, I hope I'm not too late: I'd never forgive myself if it went down the spout.

DARBISHIRE: Do you want the pliers?

JENNINGS: No, I'll use my fingers. Oh, gosh! It's gone... No, wait, I've got it – hooray!

DARBISHIRE: Hooray!

TEMPLE: Bring it in quick. Let's have a look at it!

JENNINGS: Here you are: it should be all... Oh, gosh, what's happened to it? It- it isn't black any more – it's red!

Reaction from boys

DARBISHIRE: But that's impossible! We all three saw how black it was!

TEMPLE: If you ask me, there's been some hanky-panky: that stamp's a forgery – as soon as it's given a scientific chemical test in a puddle of water, it turns red. You're a hornswoggler, Jennings – trying to get five shillings out of me on false pretences.

JENNINGS: But, dash it, Temple, it wasn't us: we didn't know it was just a brilliant forgery. Look, we'll make a reduction and let you have it for four and six.

TEMPLE: You've got a hope! Those Victorian reds are only worth twopence.

DARBISHIRE: But if you won't give us the five shillings, what are we going to do?

TEMPLE: That's your headache. (*fading*) I'm going to get ready for tea.

JENNINGS: You know what this means, Darbishire? S. Boddington is a fraud, and I shouldn't be surprised if the other S. Boddington wasn't as well. When they're weighed in the balances, they're found wanting.

DARBISHIRE: Found wanting what?

JENNINGS: Wanting five shillings for illegal forgeries: that's twice we've been chiselled. I've got a good mind to write and tell them what we think of them.

DARBISIHRE: Yes, let's do it right away and say we're sorry about not being able to send them... I say, Jen, this lets us out of paying that five bob. They can't expect us to fork out for a scientifically proved forgery.

JENNINGS: No, of course not; and they won't try to make us pay, in case we expose them as frauds. I say, how wizard! Let's get on with the letter. I've got a sheet of notepaper and an envelope in my desk. (*Desk lid bangs*) Here we are.

DARBISHIRE: I'll write it. I'll say, "Dear Mr. S&S Boddington."

JENNINGS: I bet this letter makes them sit up! You know, Darbi, we ought to get a reward for this. It isn't every day of the week a firm of unscrupulous forgers are unmasked. Let them have it, hot and strong: don't spare their feelings.

DARBISHIRE: Okay – I won't.

JENNINGS: What have you put so far?

DARBISHIRE: "Dear Mr. S&S Boddington – I hope you are quite well."

JENNINGS: What! But you great prehistoric remains, what do you want to hope that for?

DARBISHIRE: I always start off my letters that way.

JENNINGS: I said you'd got to be tough with them: you'd better start again.

DARBISHIRE: I haven't got any more notepaper.

JENNINGS: You'll have to alter it then. Let's think. "I hope you are"... I know – you could make it – "I hope you are quite well aware that your Penny Black is a dud, and if you think

48

we are going to send you five shillings for a free packet of crooked stamps, you've got a cheek. And what's more, I think Mr. S. Boddington is a crook, or if he isn't, the other Mr. S. Boddington probably is. With best wishes from your Obedient Customers."

DARBISHIRE: Hi, half a mo – I can't write shorthand. I'll just put…

VENABLES: (*approaching*) Oh, there you arc, Darbishire. Where's that piece of cake you promised me?

DARBISHIRE: Don't interrupt, Venables, I'm busy.

VENABLES: Yes, but what about my cake?

JENNINGS: Cake? Oh, yes, of course, Darbi promised you a slice. Well, that's all off now, isn't it, Darbi?

DARBISHIRE: Yes, I'm afraid so.

VENABLES: Gosh, I like that: why?

JENNINGS: Well, you see, we *had* decided to be specially decent to you, because you gave us the stamps back, but one of them was a dud, so there's no point in our going on being decent to you now, is there?

VENABLES: Well, I like the cheek of that!

DARBISHIRE: Well, it *is* rather a waste of decency, isn't it? And a waste of cake, too, of course. All the same, Jen, we *could* go on being decent to him without actually giving him any cake, couldn't we? Because, we do owe him something.

JENNINGS: I don't see that: Venables has let us down badly. We thought he was generously forking out a rare penny stamp, and all the time it wasn't worth twopence.

VENABLES: I don't know what you're talking about. What's all this about penny stamps worth twopence?

JENNINGS: Oh, it's just a rare forgery we've discovered. We found a Penny Black among those stamps we gave you, and when we gave it a scientific chemical test in the gutter spout, all the black came off.

VENABLES: Yes, I thought perhaps it would.

JENNINGS: So what we're going to… I say, what did you say then?

VENABLES: I said I thought it might wash off.

DARBISHIRE: You mean you knew about it?

VENABLES: Well, of course: I painted it!

JENNINGS: What!

VENABLES: Yes, why not? It was only a cheap red one, and I wanted to try out my new paint box.

DARBISHIRE: Oh, golly, that means the Boddingtons aren't the double dyed villains we took them for.

JENNINGS: It means more than that, Darbi: it means we'll have to send them that five shillings after all!

DARBISHIRE: But we haven't got it.

JENNINGS: I know... of course, I've got two half-crown books of stamps in my writing case – ordinary ones I mean.

DARBISHIRE: Why on earth didn't you say so before: they'll do wizardly. After all, they collect stamps, don't they?

JENNINGS: Not unused English ones. Sending stamps to a firm of philasterisks is just like sending coals to Newcastle.

DARBISHIRE: It's the best we can do. I'll go and borrow some more writing paper, then we'll pop the half-crown books inside... Oh, gosh! We won't have one left over to put on the envelope.

VENABLES: That's all right; you can get one from Mr. Wilkins: he's in charge of dishing out stamps.

JENNINGS: It's not so easy as all that, Venables. You see, we've just had a bit of a hoo-hah with Old Wilkie about stamps.

DARBISHIRE: I expect it'll be all right, Jen. Just explain things briefly in a nutshell.

MR. WILKINS: (*approaching*) Come along, hurry up, you boys. It's time you were getting ready for tea.

DARBISHIRE: Here he is now. Go on, Jennings – ask him.

JENNINGS: I don't really like to: er – sir, Mr. Wilkins, sir?

MR. WILKINS: What is it now, Jennings? I warn you, I've had just about enough of your nonsense for one day.

JENNINGS: This isn't nonsense: we want a stamp, sir.

MR. WILKINS: If you think I've got stamps to spare for picking up with pliers... and chasing with butterfly nets...

JENNINGS: Oh, it's not like that this time, sir. We really have got a letter to post now, sir. You see – well, I don't quite know how to explain.

MR. WILKINS: Hurry up, boy, hurry up! The tea bell's gone.

JENNINGS: Well, to put it in a nut-shell, sir. What we've got to do is rather like sending coals to Newcastle.

MR. WILKINS: Don't talk such arrant balderdash, boy. If you really want me to post a letter – all right, bring it up to my room after tea, but I warn you, Jennings, if you're expecting me to send coals to Newcastle in a nut-shell, I'll... I'll... well, you'd better look out.

Fade out. Music.

Dear David,

Last week Darbishire and I did someone a
decent turn and what was the result? I will not
tell you yet in case your nerves are not strong,
but it does prove that some grown-up men of what
is called advanced years, or even only fairly
advanced - these people have just got no idea of
school rules. And when they think they are being
decent, they aren't, and will not listen. It was
hard luck, too, because I had thought of a
supersonic wheeze which was an idea in a
thousand, or even in a million; or if it was not
that, at any rate it was an idea.

Blotch is scarce at present, so will stop now
as I can't turn over, but will tell you all about
it on Wed.

Yours affeckly,

J.C.T. Jennings.

JENNINGS
TO THE RESCUE

(Fourth series no.3)

Jennings to the Rescue was the twenty-third Jennings play.

It was first broadcast by the BBC Home Service for Children's Hour on 5th December 1951, with the following cast:

JENNINGS	John Charlesworth
DARBISHIRE	Henry Searle
VENABLES	Patrick Wells
TEMPLE	Malcolm Hillier
MR. CARTER }	
BOATMAN }	Geoffrey Wincott
THE HEADMASTER	Edgar Norfolk
MR. FEATHERSTONEHAUGH	Felix Felton
MRS. FEATHERSTONEHAUGH	Patience Collier

Produced by David Davis

Fade in background of excited voices

VENABLES: (*approaching*) Keep the gangway clear, you chaps. Mr. Carter's coming along with the list of the team against Bracebridge.

TEMPLE: Oh, wizzo! That means the match is on after all. Mr. Carter said he might have to cancel it if the rain didn't stop.

JENNINGS: Well, it *has* stopped; the sun's coming out now. Here's me scoring a famous goal against Bracebridge – pheew-wham!

VENABLES: What makes you so sure you're playing this afternoon, Jennings?

JENNINGS: Well, I've got a good chance, Venables. There's no harm in hoping, is there?

VENABLES: Perhaps not, but... well, what are you hanging about for, Darbishire? You won't be in the team even if Jennings is. They wouldn't pick you if you were the last man on earth.

DARBISHIRE: No, I don't suppose they would; if I was the last man on earth there'd be no one left for me to play against.

TEMPLE: Mind out, Darbishire, here comes Mr. Carter. Are you going to pin the team up, sir?

MR. CARTER: I am, Temple; if you'll step out of my way.

OMNES: Oh, wizzo. Super-socko-sonic. Hope I'm playing!

VENABLES: Would you like to borrow my drawing pin, sir?

MR. CARTER: No, thank you, Venables. There you are... Now, listen to me. Those who are playing will have to change straight away – there isn't much time. I couldn't announce the team earlier because the weather was so doubtful.

TEMPLE: Who's playing, Venables? Read it out; I can't see from here.

VENABLES: "Linbury Court Second Eleven versus Bracebridge School, at home"... Yes, you're playing, Temple; so am I. Atkinson is inside-right and – Oh, bad luck, Jennings. You're not playing. You've had it this time.

JENNINGS: Looks like it, doesn't it? Sir, Mr. Carter, sir, do you want any twelfth men or anything like that?

MR. CARTER: I'm afraid not, Jennings. I've left you out because Matron doesn't think you are fit enough, after that bad cold you had last week.

JENNINGS: Yes, I see, sir. Good thing it's only a Home Match: I'd have been a bit fed up if it had been on their ground,

54

because they always give you a smashing tea at Bracebridge.

MR. CARTER: I expect you will be able to find some other way of spending your half holiday.

JENNINGS: Yes – what can we do, Darbishire?

DARBISHIRE: How would it be if – I know, sir; will you give us permission to go for an expedition, so's we can do some bird watching?

JENNINGS: Oh, yes, please, sir; that'd be wizard. We could go down by the river, couldn't we, Darbi?

MR. CARTER: I have no objection to that, Jennings, provided you don't go *on* the river.

JENNINGS: Thank you, sir. Come along, Darbi: let's get our coats and go right away.

VENABLES: (*calling*) Oh, sir, Mr. Carter, sir?

MR. CARTER: What is it, Venables?

VENABLES: Please, sir, I've got a nail in my football boot, sir?

MR. CARTER: Why on earth do you leave it to the last moment before you find these things out?

VENABLES: But what shall I do, sir? It's a massive great nail. It feels as high as the Eiffel Tower when you put your toe on it, sir.

MR. CARTER: Go and see if Mr. Wilkins can cope with it. I can't spare the time now. I'm just going in to see the headmaster.

VENABLES: Yes, sir.

Music

Door knock

HEADMASTER: Come in! (*Door opens*) Ah, come in, Carter.

MR. CARTER: You want to see me, sir?

HEADMASTER: Yes, it's about this afternoon's match against Bracebridge. The groundsman's just been along to say that the last heavy shower during lunch has made our pitch so wet that it is inadvisable to play on it.

MR. CARTER: Oh dear, that's a pity. I've just this moment announced the team. I'm glad you told me though, because if we've got to cancel the match, I'd better get Bracebridge on the phone right away. They'll be starting off in a few minutes.

HEADMASTER: You'd better use my phone then.

MR. CARTER: Thank you, sir. (*Receiver picked up*) "Dunhambury 153, please"... It's too bad about the pitch. The sun's coming out, now it's too late... "Hello, is that Bracebridge School? Mr. Parkinson? This is Carter here, of Linbury Court. I'm afraid we shall have to cancel the match this afternoon. Our ground is unusable after this morning's rain... What's that? Yes, I think we could manage it. Hold on a moment"... They suggest we play the match on their ground, sir: it's not so wet as ours.

HEADMASTER: Very well, Carter. Tell them we'll be over in half an hour.

MR. CARTER: (*into phone*) "Hello, that's all right, then. We'll bring the team along at half-past two. Goodbye."

(*Receiver hung up*)

HEADMASTER: That means I'd better come along as well. I can take six in my car with a squash, and you can get the rest in yours. There won't be much room. I hope you haven't put too many bulky boys in the team this time, Carter?

MR. CARTER: I don't think so: here's the list.

HEADMASTER: H'm! You're not playing Jennings today, I notice?

MR. CARTER: No, Matron didn't think it was wise. He's very disappointed, of course.

HEADMASTER: He would be: he's very keen. I wonder if we could squeeze him into one of the cars and take him over to Bracebridge to watch?

MR. CARTER: Too late I'm afraid, sir. I gave him and Darbishire permission to go for a walk by the river. I expect they'll be half way there by now.

Fade to rippling water

DARBISHIRE: (*fade in*) Well, I don't call this much of an expedition, Jennings. We've been sitting here on the bank for about a hundred years and we haven't seen a whisker of a bird yet: the only thing to look at is that notice just along the bank - "Rowing Boats for Hire, two shillings per person per hour."

JENNINGS: I know. Wouldn't it be smashing!

DARBISHIRE: What – to take a boat on the river?

JENNINGS: Yes, if *only* it wasn't strictly against school rules. Still, it's out of the question: let's forget about it... er – you don't happen to have enough money on you, in any case, I suppose?

DARBISHIRE: I've got two shillings, that's all, and anyway it would be four shillings for the two of us.

JENNINGS: Well, that wipes it out completely, then. After all, rules are rules, aren't they? ...er – do you think they would let us have a boat for a shilling per person per half-of-per-hour, perhaps? There's the boatman: he's just hauling a boat in now. Let's go and see what he says.

DARBISHIRE: I don't think we ought to. Suppose the Head or someone came for a walk along the river bank – what then?

JENNINGS: How could he? There's a Home Match on today, isn't there? Very well, then, the staff will all be watching that. Come along, I'm going to ask him...

Fade out/fade in

Excuse me, have you a boat for hire?

BOATMAN: Just one left, son. Here you are. Four shillings an hour for the two of you.

JENNINGS: I know, that's the trouble. Could we pay part of the payment per part of the time, do you think?

DARBISHIRE: He means a shilling per half of per person per half of per hour, if you follow me.

BOATMAN: Suits me: bring the boat back by three o'clock and I'll only charge you two shillings.

JENNINGS: Oh, that's awfully decent of you.

DARBISHIRE: You know, Jen, I'm not sure we ought to go on with this. I'm not terribly good at managing boats – practically a landlubber as you might say, and the shipping forecast was not at all good this morning. Gales in Iceland, Faroes, Fair Isle, Hebrides, Cromarty, Forties and...

BOATMAN: Don't you worry, son, you'll barely get out of sight and back in half an hour, let alone row to Iceland. Step in while I hold the boat steady (*effect*) – hey, I said *step* in, not jump in. This 'ere's a rowing boat, not a submarine.

JENNINGS: Yes, don't be such a clumsy grid-iron, Darbishire. We don't want to land up in Davey Jones's Locker before we get started.

BOATMAN: In you go, then. Now who's going to row?

JENNINGS: }

DARBISHIRE: } I am.

JENNINGS: Well, I can row, Darbi, and you can't.

DARBISHIRE: Yes, but it's my two shillings, so it's only fair to let me have a bash.

BOATMAN: That's settled, then. Take an oar apiece.

Oars in rowlocks

JENNINGS: Right, cast away!

BOATMAN: Hoy! It's only a suggestion like, but if you're both going to row, it'd help matters considerable if you was both facing the same way.

JENNINGS: Yes, of course: you are an ignorant bazooka, Darbishire. Surely you know you have to sit facing backwards if you want to row forwards.

DARBISHIRE: I can't sit facing backwards: I get a crick in the neck.

JENNINGS: Turn round then... careful!

BOATMAN: Off you go then.

Splash of rowing

DARBISHIRE: Gosh, this is good fun, isn't it? I never realised rowing was so easy. All you've got to do is to – I say, Jen, are we in a whirlpool or something? We're swirling round in circles like a cyclone.

JENNINGS: You're not pulling, that's why. We've got to go more to starboard.

DARBISHIRE: Which side's that?

JENNINGS: It's the same as the starboard engine of an aircraft.

DARBISHIRE: Oh, that's easy then. I thought perhaps boats were opposite...

Rowing

I say, are you sure they're not opposite? We're still spinning like a gramophone record.

JENNINGS: Pull on your oar, then – no, don't pull it out of the water. Oh, gosh, you are hopeless, Darbi! Pull harder your side. We're not nearly starboard enough yet.

DARBISHIRE: Starboard! Let me see, that's opposite to the way we're going, isn't it?

JENNINGS: I've told you about fifty million times already: it's the same as an aeroplane. Honestly, Darbi, it's a waste of time telling you anything. It just goes in one ear and out of the other, like water off a duck's back.

DARBISHIRE: That doesn't make sense. What's a duck's back got to do with starboard engines?

JENNINGS: Nothing, you bogus ruin: it's just a saying. If you pour water on a duck's back it runs off.

DARBISHIRE: I don't blame it: so would anyone if you did that to them.

JENNINGS: I don't mean the duck runs off – I mean the water.

DARBISHIRE: Oh, I see. I say, we're not doing so badly. We've come a long way already.

JENNINGS: We're going down-stream, that's why: and there's a supersonic current running. It's going to be pretty tricky rowing back against it.

DARBISHIRE: Golly, yes: we ought to have gone up the river to start with.

JENNINGS: That's just what I was trying to do, but with you splashing about like a performing sea-lion, we've been doing a one-way traffic act in the wrong direction. Come on now for goodness' sake!...

Fade out/fade in. Distant church clock striking three / Rowing

DARBISHIRE: (*fade in*) Oh, fish-hooks, there's three o'clock striking already and we're miles from the boathouse. Whatever's the boatman going to say when we tell him we can't pay for our overtime?

JENNINGS: I don't know: we mustn't let this become front page news, whatever happens. If only you could row just a leetle straighter.

Drop oars

DARBISHIRE: It's no good, Jen, I need more practice. We might get on better if you rowed and I sat in the narrow end and navigated for you.

JENNINGS: Righto – give me your oar and nip into the bows.

DARBISHIRE: I don't think I ought to move about while the boat's out of its depth. It's a bit tippity; – and my father says you should never change horses in mid-stream.

JENNINGS: You aren't changing horses – you're changing places. Why start bringing horses in – it's as much as we can do to manage an eight-foot dinghy.

DARBISHIRE: Oh, there isn't a horse really, any more than there was a duck when you made water run in one of its ears and off its back. What my father means is, that if you're on a horse...

JENNINGS: Look out, Darbi – look out!

DARBISHIRE: Look out where?

JENNINGS: Starboard bow – coming round the bend. There's a big man in a small skiff heading straight for us. (*calling*) Hoy!... Hoy! Oh gosh, he's got his back to us and he can't see where he's going... Hoy, there – look out!...

DARBISHIRE: He's seen us, look; he's back-pedalling.

JENNINGS: Too late; he'll never stop in time. Oh, gosh, we're going to collide broadside... Help! Help!

Boats collide, splash

DARBISHIRE: Oh, golly, what's happening: are we all right?

JENNINGS: Yes, *we* are, but the skiff isn't. It's capsized; there's this chap in the water, look. Come on, Darbi, row like mad to the rescue.

DARBISHIRE: But I can only row round and round, and it's no good rowing in circles, however madly.

MR. F'HAUGH: (*off*) Help, help, ahoy there! Attention all shipping.

JENNINGS: Come on, Darbi: swing the boat round and we'll be able to reach him.

MR. F'HAUGH: Help, help! (*spluttering*) Ach!... Gll!... Pff!

DARBISHIRE: Quick – he's sinking! He can't swim!

MR. F'HAUGH: I tell you I *can* swim; I had six lessons last – ach... gll... pff... You're quite right – I can't swim. Those six lessons weren't quite enough. (*gasping ad lib*) Ach!... gll!... pff!

JENNINGS: (*calls*) All right, we're coming... (*close*) Give me your hand – I've got you. I'll pull you into the boat.

DARBISHIRE: Look out, Jennings; we'll capsize if you lean over any more. You can't possibly get him over the side.

JENNINGS: We'll trail him behind us then, like a harpooned whale. You hold his hand and I'll row to the bank.

DARBISHIRE: Okay: I've got him. Are you all right?

JENNINGS:)   Yes.

MR. F'HAUGH:)   No.

JENNINGS: Nearly there... (*Splashing, rowing, gasping ad lib till boat grounds*) Here we are. I'll get out first, Darbi; then we can haul him in.

MR. F'HAUGH: All right – all right – all right: I can manage for myself.

Sounds of disembarking

DARBISHIRE: Gosh, that was a near squeak! Are you all right?

MR. F'HAUGH: Of course I am. I've just said so three times. Sorry about the collision though; my fault entirely. Wasn't looking where I was going. Now where's my skiff?

MR. F'HAUGH: I think I can reach it; the rope's trailing in the water... (*he reaches for it*) Got it: good!

DARBISHIRE: And here's your hat, bobbing about. I think I can reach it with this oar... That's it – got it!

MR. F'HAUGH: Splendid. We'll tie both the boats up and then go indoors. That's my house, just up the bank. Brr! It's cold.

DARBISHIRE: Oh, but we can't stay: we've got to take our boat back, and we haven't got any money to pay for the overtime.

MR. F'HAUGH: That's all right: I'll settle it with the boatman. Old friend of mine. He won't worry. Now, first, I must express my heartfelt thanks to you for coming to my rescue. A most courageous act carried out in the face of great personal danger.

JENNINGS: It was nothing, really.

MR. F'HAUGH: (*shivering and chattering teeth throughout sequence*) Of course, it wasn't nothing really. If I say your action was – brr! Gallant – then it was – brr! – gallant. Of course if the water hadn't been so icy, I should have been able to struggle out, but when it's as cold as that, I just curl up and can't swim.

DARBISHIRE: "Stickly prickly, that's him."

MR. F'HAUGH: That's who?

DARBISHIRE: It's just a quotation you reminded me of:
                "Curls up and can't swim –
                Stickly prickly, that's him."

He's a hedgehog, you see.

MR. F'HAUGH: And why should I remind you of a hedgehog?

DARBISHIRE: You don't really: he's just a character in one of Rudyard Kipling's stories.

MR. F'HAUGH: Just so! But that's neither here nor there: come along up to the house before I catch my death of cold. There's no point in saving me from drowning to let me perish of frostbite.

DARBISHIRE: We really must be going if you'll excuse us.

MR. F'HAUGH: I will not excuse you: you can't go yet. I don't even know who you are.

JENNINGS: I'm Jennings and this is Darbishire: we're at boarding school near here.

MR. F'HAUGH: Excellent! My name's Mr. Hum-Humphrey F-f-ee...

JENNINGS: I say, your teeth are in a bad way, aren't they? They're chattering like magpies.

MR. F'HAUGH: I'm Hum-Humphrey F-f-fee...

DARBISHIRE: Don't bother: I can see your name on your hat – Mr. Feather-stone-haw.

MR. F'HAUGH: No, it's nothing of the sort.

DARBISHIRE: You mean, this isn't your hat?

MR. F'HAUGH: I mean that's not the way to pronounce my name. It's spelt Featherstonehaugh, but it's pronounced Feestonhay: like Cholmondeley pronounced Chumley.

DARBISHIRE: Or Durbyshire pronounced Darbishire.

MR. F'HAUGH: Yes, that's right.

JENNINGS: Or Festival of Britain, pronounced Success.

MR. F'HAUGH: Eh?

JENNINGS: It was just headline I saw in the paper. I thought it was a bit queer at the time.

Fade out/fade in

MR. F'HAUGH: Here we are... And there's my wife at the back door.

MRS. F'HAUGH: (*off*) Good gracious, Humphrey.   Whatever's happened?

MR. F'HAUGH: Don't start fussing, Amanda. All's well. Come along in you boys. Now, Amanda, I want to introduce...

MRS. F'HAUGH: Oh, but Humphrey, you're all wet!

MR. F'HAUGH: Oh course I am! *You* take a header into the river and come out dry if you think it's so easy. These two brave boys have just rescued me from a watery tomb.

MRS. F'HAUGH: Oh, but how splendid of them!

MR. F'HAUGH: Just what I thought myself. Jennings and Darbishire – this is my wife.

JENNINGS: How do you do, Mrs. Chumley, - I mean Mrs. – er...

MRS. F'HAUGH: Mrs. Feestonhay, dear; not spelt like that, of course. It's like Beauchamp, pronounced Beecham.

JENNINGS: Oh, is it?

MRS. F'HAUGH: Is it what, dear?

JENNINGS: Is it pronounced Beecham?

MRS. F'HAUGH: No dear, it's pronounced Feestonhay.

JENNINGS: Oh! Well, why is it spelt Chumley?

DARBISHIRE: I don't think you understand, Jennings. My father says that the origin of surnames is...

MR. F'HAUGH: A-a-achoo!

MRS. F'HAUGH: Oh, Humphrey, you sneezed! You're catching cold.

MR. F'HAUGH: Of course, I am, Achoo! You don't think it was a-a-a – false alarm – you didn't think it was hay fever, did you? I'm going upstairs to put some dry clothes on, then I'll run these boys back to school in the car and tell their headmaster of their outstanding gallantry and self-sacrifice. He'll be a proud man when he hears what his boys have been up to this afternoon.

JENNINGS: Oh, no, please don't do that: you mustn't tell the Head, really. We're not allowed on the river.

MR. F'HAUGH: Nonsense: the trouble with you is you're too modest. A heroic deed of this nature must not go unrecognised. I feel this is an occasion that demands a-a-achoo!

MRS. F'HAUGH: Do go up and change, Humphrey dear, while I make a nice cup of tea in the kitchen. Tut! You're dripping all over the carpet.

MR. F'HAUGH: I'm going now. I shan't be long, then I'll get the car out and we'll be off to tell your headmaster all about it, eh?

Exeunt the F'Haughs ad lib / Fade out / fade in

DARBISHIRE: Oh, gosh, this is frantic. What on earth's the Head going to say. He'll be as livid as a brace of coots when he hears we've been on the river, and it's just no good trying to explain about school rules to these people. I say, do you think we could beat it out of the back door before he's finished changing?

JENNINGS: No, not with old mother Chumley-Bo-chump on guard in the kitchen. We've had it this time, Darbi. In ten minutes or so, we'll be bowling up the drive to the Head's study, and then... Darbi, I've got it: the most supersonic wheeze in history!

DARBISHIRE: What?

JENNINGS: Well, we haven't told him yet which school we go to, so all we've got to do is to take him to the wrong one.

DARBISHIRE: Oh, talk sense, Jen: there isn't a wrong one.

JENNINGS: We'll direct him to Bracebridge School instead of Linbury. Then, when he beetles in to find the Head, we can nip out of the car and beat it back to Linbury on foot.

DARBISHIRE: Oh, massive idea, supersockosonic! I say, Jennings, you *have* got a brain. How do you think these marvellous schemes out?

JENNINGS: Oh, I don't know, it's just a gift, I suppose: ssh! There's someone coming.

Door opens/shuts

MR. F'HAUGH: (*approaching*) Didn't take me long to change, eh? That's me all over. Never waste time. I'll go and get the car out and we'll be off, right away. I've got another appointment in half an hour and I don't want to be late for it. Come along through the kitchen to the garage.

(Door opens, calling)

Just taking these lads back to school, Amanda.

MRS. F'HAUGH: Oh, but Humphrey, I haven't made the tea yet and I

63

did promise them…

MR. F'HAUGH: Can't wait for that now, Amanda.   What's a cup of tea, anyway?   Why, when their headmaster hears what I've got to tell him, he'll feed them on turkey and ice-cream for the rest of the term, eh?   Come along you boys!

JENNINGS: Goodbye Mrs. – Chum – er – Feestonhay.   Thank you for nearly getting us some tea.

MRS. F'HAUGH: Goodbye, dears; and next time you're out for a row, be sure to come and see us, won't you?

DARBISHIRE: Thanks very much, but somehow I don't think we'll be on the river for a long time.

Exeunt ad lib / fade / Car engine starts

MR. F'HAUGH: Come along.   Jump in, jump in.   (*Car door slam, car moves off*)   Now then, which way do we go?

JENNINGS: You're sure you've really *got* to take us back, I suppose?   I mean, we'd much rather you didn't.

MR. F'HAUGH: Nonsense, I won't hear of such a thing.

JENNINGS: In that case, you'd better turn left at the end of this road, then right at the top of the hill till you see a big – I *think* it's a red brick building.

DARBISHIRE: No, it isn't, Jen, it's grey stone with a brass plate outside.

JENNINGS: Is it?   I can't remember.

MR. F'HAUGH: Not very observant, are you?   Ought to know what you own school looks like.

JENNINGS: Well anyway, the important thing is to see that it's got "Bracebridge School" written up outside

MR. F'HAUGH: Bracebridge School?   Right: we shan't be long now.

Engine revs up / fade / cross fade in cheers at football match

Referee's final whistle / cheers fade / background schoolboy chatter

VENABLES: Jolly good game, wasn't it, Temple?

TEMPLE: Super: that second goal of yours, Venables – smashing shot.   Let's go and see what Mr. Carter thought about it. There he is, look, talking to the Head on the touch-line.

VENABLES: We'd better not disturb them now, Temple.   They're too busy nattering: let's go and change.   I'm glad we had to play on this ground.   They give you a wizard tea at Bracebridge, you know.

Car horn: off

TEMPLE: Mind out!   There's a car coming.   You'll get run over.

VENABLES: Must be one of their masters – yes, it is; he's got two boys in the back.   Come on, let's go and get ready for… Gosh, Temple, they're not Bracebridge chaps at all in that

64

car... it's Jennings and Darbishire!

TEMPLE: What! Yes, you're right! They're pulling up. Let's go and find out what they've come over here for.

They go, ad lib

MR. F'HAUGH: (*approach*) Now, you two boys wait by the car while I go and find the headmaster. I don't think I've met him before. What does he look like?

JENNINGS: He's... well, I don't really know.

MR. F'HAUGH: You don't know? But you must know! Is he tall or short, young or old.

JENNINGS: I should say he's – well... tall and dark, wouldn't you, Darbishire?

DARBISHIRE: Ye-es: if anything, rather on the short side though, with fair hair and quite old.

JENNINGS: I should have said he was a bit youngish myself.

MR. F'HAUGH: That's very helpful, I must say. I've got to look for a tall, dark, young man, who's a short elderly blonde. (*going*) I'll go and ring the bell and make my own enquiries, thank you.

JENNINGS: Well, that's got rid of him, thank goodness. Now we can hoof off, and... Gosh, Darbi, look – there's Venables and Temple. What on earth...?

VENABLES: (*approaching*) I say, Jennings, what on earth are you and Darbi doing here?

JENNINGS: I was going to ask you that first.

TEMPLE: We came to play the match, of course.

JENNINGS: But the match was at home.

TEMPLE: It *was* to have been, but our ground was too muddy, so they switched it. Didn't you know? Mr. Carter brought half the team over in his old crock and Venables and I came in the Archbeako's car.

JENNINGS: In the...! You don't mean the Head's over here now, do you?

VENABLES: Yes, there he is strolling round the pitch with Mr. Carter.

DARBISHIRE: Oh, my hat, what a frantic bish! We came here specially because we knew he wouldn't be here. It would have been much better, Jen if we'd told Mr. Feestonhay to take us straight back to Linbury. The Head would have been out, and perhaps we could have got rid of him before he came back.

JENNINGS: There's still time if we're lucky. We'll try to get him to take us away before he and the Archbeako make contact.

VENABLES: But what's it all about?

DARBISHIRE: Oh, he's just a character we did a good turn to, and he wants to repay our kindness by telling the Head all about it.

TEMPLE: Well, why not?

JENNINGS: Huh! If we hadn't been out of bounds on the river in a hired boat we couldn't finish paying for, we shouldn't have *done* him the good turn.

VENABLES: Oh, goodness, you are up a gum tree! Who is this chap, anyway?

JENNINGS: Well, his name's Feather-stone-haugh really, but it's spelt Chumley and pronounced Beecham.

TEMPLE: Look out, he's coming back. (*going*) We'd better clear off, Venables.

MR. F'HAUGH: (*approaching*) Doesn't anybody ever answer the front door in this school? I can't hang about all day. I've got another appointment soon. Where is this headmaster of yours, Jennings?

JENNINGS: Yes, well, I'm awfully sorry, Mr. Featherstonehaugh, but there's been a bit of a bish. We've come to the wrong school!

MR. F'HAUGH: We've done *what*!

DARBISHIRE: Yes, we were rather led astray by appearances and...

MR. F'HAUGH: But, good heavens, laddie! Surely you know which school you go to, don't you?

JENNINGS: Yes, but –

MR. F'HAUGH: Then don't talk such nonsense. I've had enough of this self-effacing modesty. I'm in a hurry and I want to speak to your headmaster before I go, whether he's here or not. Now, who are those two men walking round the football pitch over there? Is one of them your headmaster?

DARBISHIRE: Yes it is, but I'd rather you...

MR. F'HAUGH: Oh, it is, is it? Well, why on earth didn't you say so before, instead of letting me waste my time ringing door bells. You wait here while I drive over and have a word with him.

Car starts, fades out. Pause. Fades in

HEADMASTER: I still think we should have won that match, Carter, if the halves had backed up the forwards a bit better.

MR. CARTER: You're probably right, sir. It was a pity we had to leave Jennings out: he makes quite a difference to the team.

HEADMASTER: Quite.

MR. CARTER: I think Parkinson's expecting us for tea in the drawing-room. The boys will be having theirs in the dining

hall when they've changed and... (*car* hoots) I think this
gentleman wants a word with you.

MR. F'HAUGH: (*approaching*) Good afternoon: my name's
Feestonhay. I understand you're the headmaster?

MR. CARTER: No, I'm afraid not: my name's Carter.

MR. F'HAUGH: Oh, then *you* must be the headmaster here, and I
should like to congratulate you upon the courageous
conduct...

HEADMASTER: One moment: I'm not the headmaster of Bracebridge.

MR. F'HAUGH: You're not? One of the boys just told me you were!
This is ridiculous. First they don't know which school they
go to, and now they don't recognise their own headmaster
when they see him.

HEADMASTER: I think I see where the mistake has arisen. I am *a*
headmaster, but not *the* headmaster.

MR. F'HAUGH: Just how many headmasters has this school got?

HEADMASTER: No, you misunderstand. We are visitors here. The
man you want is Mr. Parkinson. I doubt whether he's
available at the moment.

MR. F'HAUGH: Well, I've no time to wait for him if he isn't. You
won't be seeing him by any chance?

MR. CARTER: Oh, yes, we're on our way to his drawing-room now.

MR. F'HAUGH: Then perhaps you'll be good enough to tell him that
two of his boys have just saved me from a watery tomb. I
was on the river this afternoon and my skiff accidentally
collided with a hired dinghy which was being rowed by two
Bracebridge boys. They rescued me with considerable verve
and aplomb.

HEADMASTER: Really? Highly commendable behaviour.

MR. F'HAUGH: It certainly was, and I think the recognition of this
valiant act is called for. Now tell me – if they had been your
boys, what reward would you give them?

HEADMASTER: Well, my boys are not allowed on the river, so the
circumstances could not possibly arise. But were I the
headmaster of an establishment where unsupervised rowing
formed a part of the curriculum – as presumably it does here
at Bracebridge – then I should certainly reward such conduct
with a half-holiday – yes, quite definitely a half-holiday.

MR. F'HAUGH: Just what I thought myself. I can't stop any longer,
but I should be most grateful if you will tell the appropriate
headmaster what's happened.

HEADMASTER: Certainly I will.

MR. F'HAUGH: And don't forget the half-holiday.

HEADMASTER: Ha, ha! No, of course not: that's most important. Well, goodbye, Mr. Feestonhay.

MR. F'HAUGH: (*Fading*) Goodbye – goodbye!

Car engine starts

MR. CARTER: One moment; you haven't told us the names of these boys? Mr. Parkinson will want to know who they are.

MR. F'HAUGH: (*off*) Yes, of course. One was called Jennings and the other one Darbishire. Goodbye.

Car fades to distance

HEADMASTER: Jennings and Darbishire! Jennings and Darbishire! That *was* what he said, wasn't it, Carter?

MR. CARTER: He certainly did.

HEADMASTER: That means those boys have been on the river, which is strictly against school rules. As soon as I return to Linbury, I shall send for them and... Bless my soul! Carter, can I believe my eyes!

MR. CARTER: Good heavens, yes! There they are! Well, well! Shall I call them over, sir?

HEADMASTER: Yes, do.

MR. CARTER: (*Calling*) Jennings and Darbishire!

JENNINGS: Sir?

MR. CARTER: Come over here.

HEADMASTER: You know, Carter, this breach of school rules is extremely serious and I'm prepared to be very terse about it – very terse indeed, after which I shall punish them severely.

MR. CARTER: Yes, sir – and after that?

HEADMASTER: After that? I don't follow, Carter?

MR. CARTER: After you've punished them, will you grant the half-holiday which you agree with Mr. Feestonhay was a fitting reward for meritorious conduct?

HEADMASTER: Oh, but surely, Carter, considering the circumstances, I – yes, I did approve in principle of a half-holiday, I must confess.

MR. CARTER: You suggested it yourself, sir.

HEADMASTER: I know I did, but...

JENNINGS: (*approaching*) Yes, sir; you sent for us, sir.

HEADMASTER: I did, Jennings. And do you know why?

JENNINGS: Yes, sir. Because we went on the river, sir.

HEADMASTER: Precisely, Jennings.

DARBISHIRE: And we're very sorry about rescuing Mr. Feestonhay, sir, at least, I mean...

HEADMASTER: I know what you mean, Darbishire, and it places me in a difficult position. On the one hand, I have decided to punish you for breaking school rules; on the other hand, as Mr. Carter insists on reminding me, I agreed in an unguarded moment, that saving Mr. Feestonhay from his – ah – watery tomb, was an action that merited a half-holiday for the entire school. Frankly, I am at a loss how to reconcile these two opposing points of view. What are we to do, Mr. Carter?

MR. CARTER: I don't really know.

JENNINGS: I know what you *could* do, sir?

HEADMASTER: Well, Jennings, I am all ears.

JENNINGS: Well, sir, if you were to arrange the half-holiday first, sir, Darbishire and I could arrange to do something decent, like, say, for instance, a bird watching expedition. And then, just as we were going to start you could put us in detention, sir; so, we'd have our punishment but the rest of the school would be jolly grateful to us for getting them a half-holiday, sir.

HEADMASTER: A most improper suggestion, Jennings, and quite out of the question. Don't you agree, Mr. Carter?

MR. CARTER: Oh, yes, entirely – quite impossible... And yet, as it's the only practical solution, may I suggest that you announce the half-holiday after lunch tomorrow?

HEADMASTER: I – er – h'm – very well, Carter. You'd better remind me. These things have a habit of slipping my memory.

JENNINGS: }

DARBISHIRE: } Oh, thank you, sir.

HEADMASTER: And as for the detention – well, if nobody reminds me about it, there's just a chance that that may slip my memory too. Eh, Carter?

They laugh

Music.

Dear David,

Do not be alarmed at the address at the top.
I have not moved. If you are clever you will see
it is my well-known secret code I use in my diary
and you have to spell the words backwards so
nobody knows what you mean. I expect you are
stumped so I will tell you the answer is Linbury
court Preparatory School. I do not know whether
you keep a diary like Samuel Pepys and Mrs Dale
and people, but if you do, beware of writing
backwards in case the diary falls into the wrong
hands, which mine did. I will not say whose, but
just give you a clue - Retsim Snikliw.

I have asked for some blotch, but it has not
come so I will stop now but will tell you all
about it on Wed.

Yours affeckly,

J.C.T. Jennings.

JENNINGS' DIARY

(Fourth series no.4)

Jennings' Diary was the twenty-fourth Jennings play.

It was first broadcast by the BBC Home Service for Children's Hour on Wednesday, 2nd January 1952 with the following cast:

JENNINGS	John Charlesworth
DARBISHIRE	Henry Searle
MR. CARTER	Geoffrey Wincott
MR. WILKINS	Wilfred Babbage
MATRON	Virginia Winter
VENABLES	Malcolm Hillier
ATKINSON	Gawn Grainger
POLICEMAN	Ernest Sefton

Produced by David Davis

Crossfade background dormitory conversation and hold under

MATRON: Come along, Jennings: put your diary away and get undressed.

JENNINGS: (*absorbed*) Yes, Matron.

MATRON: Quickly then. You've been sitting on your bed, chewing that pencil for the last ten minutes.

JENNINGS: I know, Matron. I haven't finished writing it up yet. I can't remember what happened last Thursday.

MATRON: I should get into bed first and then write your diary, if I were you. Mr. Wilkins will be round in a few minutes to put the light out.

JENNINGS: All right, Matron. But I've wizard well got to find out what happened last Thursday, by hook or by crook. It's the only blank day I've got in my diary so far, and my Aunt Angela's promised me five shillings if I write something in it every day of the year.

MATRON: That's very generous of her.

JENNINGS: She gave it to me you see, Matron. Of course the trouble is, it's leap year. Anyone could write three hundred and sixty-*five* entries; but three hundred and sixty-*six*, well, that's the last straw, isn't it, Matron?

DARBISHIRE: (*approaching*) I say, Jennings, aren't you undressed yet?

JENNINGS: Oh, hullo, Darbishire. I'm just trying to think…

DARBISHIRE: You'd better get a move on. Old Wilkie –

MATRON: Darbishire!

DARBISHIRE: Sorry, Matron – I mean Mr. Wilkins is just coming along the corridor. He's giving us another maths test tomorrow and I… oh, there he is!

MR. WILKINS: (*gradual approach*) Hurry up you boys by the washbasins. Take a brush to those knees, Venables; you're supposed to be scrubbing them, not stroking them. Come along, Jennings and Darbishire – time you were undressed.

MATRON: Good evening, Mr. Wilkins.

MR. WILKINS: (*normal*) Good evening, Matron. By the way, I've been meaning to ask you – did any of the maids find a gold cuff-link when they cleaned my room this morning?

MATRON: A cuff-link? No, Mr. Wilkins, have you lost one?

MR. WILKINS: Yes, it was rather a nice pair, too. My sister gave them to me years ago for a twenty-first birthday present. Can't think where the thing's got to. I took them out of a shirt yesterday and I thought I put them both on my dressing-table, but one of them's completely disappeared.

MATRON: I'll go and ask the maids for you now, if you like, but I'm pretty sure they'd have brought anything like that straight to me.

MR. WILKINS: Thank you, Matron; I thought I'd mention it just in case... Jennings, will you get a move on; you're not nearly undressed yet. And when I'm talking to Matron it's very bad manners to hang about within earshot.

JENNINGS: Yes, sir. I was just thinking about your cuff-link, sir. Was it a square gold one with your initials on, sir?

MR. WILKINS: Yes; have you seen one anywhere?

JENNINGS: Yes, sir.

MR. WILKINS: Oh, good – where is it?

JENNINGS: I don't know, sir.

(Wilkins explodes)

But if they were the ones you were wearing last week, I'll know what to look out for, sir. I'll write it down in my diary, if you like, sir, so's I shan't forget.

DARBISHIRE: I'll help look, too, shall I, sir?

MR. WILKINS: That's very kind of you, Darbishire, but at the moment I'd rather you hurried into bed.

DARBISHIRE: Yes, sir... My father lost a pair of links at home once, sir, and we had to take the floorboards up to find them. Would you like me to...

MR. WILKINS: No, Darbishire. You're not taking any floorboards up in my room.

DARBISHIRE: My father found them in the end though, sir. He's got eyes like a lynx. Oh, I say, sir, did you hear that? I almost made a pun that time, didn't I, sir? I said: "My father..."

MR. WILKINS: Darbishire, if you don't' stop prattling idiotic balderdash and get into bed, I'll... I'll – well, you'd better look out. And you too, Jennings.

JENNINGS: I am, sir. I'm hurrying like blinko... Sir, were you on duty last Thursday, sir?

MR. WILKINS: No, I wasn't. Mr. Carter was.

JENNINGS: Oh, good – he'd know then, wouldn't he, sir?

MR. WILKINS: I doubt it. I hadn't lost it last Thursday.

JENNINGS: Oh, not your cuff-link, sir – I mean he'd know what happened. You see there's a blank space in my diary that's just *got* to be filled in. If I hurry up and wash super quickly, sir, may I stratocruise along to Mr. Carter's room, sir, and ask him?

MR. WILKINS: Anything that makes you hurry up and wash quickly is worth trying, Jennings. But you'd better buck up – this light's going out in five minutes.

Fade to music. Door knock

MR. CARTER: Come in.

Door opens

JENNINGS: Sir!

MR. CARTER: What is it, Jennings?

JENNINGS: Oh, sir, Mr. Carter, sir, are you busy or can you remember what happened last Thursday, sir?

MR. CARTER: Yes and no, Jennings. I *am* busy and last Thursday being my duty day I prefer to forget it. Why?

JENNINGS: Well, it's about my diary, sir. Last Thursday's just a blank chunk, and I promised my Aunt Angela I'd write something every day, even though it is Leap Year. She's going to give me five shillings if I do, and you can see how well I've kept it up so far. You can read it if you like, sir.

MR. CARTER: But isn't it a private diary?

JENNINGS: Parts of it are, sir, but the private bits are in code, so you wouldn't be able to understand them. You see if you can, sir. Here it is.

MR. CARTER: H'm! "January 1st. Fairly hot toddy... January 2nd. Not so hot toddy." You're quite safe, Jennings – I can't work out what that means.

JENNINGS: (*hurt*) Oh, but sir, that's not in code. It isn't hot toddy – it's hot *today* – the weather, sir. Aunt Angela's very keen on keeping notes about metreol... er, meteril – er, keeping notes about the weather, sir.

MR. CARTER: I see. "January 10th. Listened for cuckoo, but did not hear it." How very surprising!

JENNINGS: Yes, sir, Aunt Angela's very keen on nature and stuff, too, sir.

MR. CARTER: (*reading*) So it would appear. Yes – you've kept the entries up well enough, Jennings, but they're all so feeble that they're not worth recording. Look at this for last week. "Monday – Had bath. Tuesday – Had haircut. Wednesday –

74

Had second helping of prunes. Thursday – blank. Friday – Didn't have History test, wizzo! Saturday – Had clean socks. Broke bootlace." Surely you could think of something better than that! Why not try and write entries that are interesting to read, as the famous Samuel Pepys did in his diaries.

JENNINGS: Well, it's all very well for Pepys and people, sir, but they don't have to squeeze a whole week into a titchy little page three inches long.

MR. CARTER: No, perhaps not – now, what on earth does this mean? "Played football with SELBANEV, ERIH-SIBRAD, NOSNIKTA and Co. RETSIM RETRAC reffed the game." Sounds as though you were playing against the Moscow Dynamos.

JENNINGS: Ah, that's where the code part of it comes in, sir. It's secret, really, but I don't mind you knowing! I just write people's names the wrong way round. SELBANEV is Venables, spelled backwards, sir; ERIH-SIBRAD is Darbishire, and NOSNIKTA spells Atkinson in reverse. You spell them out, and you'll see, sir.

MR. CARTER: They sound like members of an Eastern European spy organisation to me. And who is this mysterious RETSIM RETRAC who reffed the game?

JENNINGS: RETSIM RETRAC? That's you, sir. Mister Carter spelled the wrong way round. RETSIM: that's MISTER: Mister Retrac...

Door knock/door opens. Shuts

MR. WILKINS: (*approaching*) I say, Carter, have you still got Jennings here?

MR. CARTER: He can come now, if you want him, Wilkins. He looked in to show me his diary.

MR. WILKINS: It's time he was in bed. You'll need a good night's sleep, Jennings. It's my maths test tomorrow, don't forget.

JENNINGS: Oh, yes, of course, sir. I'll go then... Oh, yes, sir, I've just remembered what happened last Thursday.

MR. CARTER: What was that?

JENNINGS: I got kept in by Mr. Wilkins for not getting enough marks in last week's test.

MR. WILKINS: (*rubbing his hands*) You'll get another chance tomorrow, Jennings. Zero hour's half-past ten!

A Mr Wilkins curtain laugh. Cross fade to music. Fade in

VENABLES: Please, sir; Mr. Wilkins, sir, I've finished that last sum.

MR. WILKINS: Good. Everybody finished?

OMNES: Yes, sir.

MR.WILKINS: You, Jennings?

JENNINGS: No, sir. I haven't actually quite got to the end of it, sir.

MR. WILKINS: And why not?

JENNINGS: Because, well, because I haven't actually quite got to the beginning of it yet, sir. I don't understand the bit about how long it takes to go from one milestone to the next at three miles an hour.

MR. WILKINS: What's difficult about that?

JENNINGS: Well, it doesn't tell you how far apart one milestone *is* from the next. I might be any distance – a mile, even!

MR. WILKINS: It not only might be – it *is*! What would be the point of having milestones that weren't a mile apart? Bring your book up, Jennings, and let me see what you've done.

JENNINGS: But I haven't written anything down yet, sir.

MR. WILKINS: You were writing something just then, when I spoke to you.

JENNINGS: That was – that was nothing much, sir.

MR. WILKINS: Do you mean to tell me that you were writing something in my lesson that wasn't what I'd set? Read it out.

JENNINGS: I couldn't sir. You wouldn't understand.

MR. WILKINS: Do as I tell you, and don't argue!

JENNINGS: Well, sir, I was writing: RETSIM SNIKLIW (*pronounce Snickloo*) G-NISSIM K-NIL.

MR. WILKINS: You were writing *what*!

JENNINGS: It's in code, sir. You see, I thought I'd make a note in my diary, about...

MR. WILKINS: Writing your diary in class! Bring it up at once. Never heard of such a thing – wasting time with nonsensical buffoonery...

JENNINGS: It isn't nonsense, sir – it's just code. I'll explain it if you like, sir.

MR. WILKINS: Give it to me... thank you. I don't want any explanations. I'm perfectly capable of... What on earth does this mean on the memorandum page? SELBANEV

SEWO EM ENO POPILLOL?

JENNINGS: You have to spell the words backwards, sir. SELBANEV is Venables and POPILLOL means lollipop. Er – the sentence means: "Venables owes me one lollipop," sir.

VENABLES: Oh, I don't sir! I paid it back last week.

MR. WILKINS: Quiet, Venables!

VENABLES: Yes, sir.

MR. WILKINS: I never heard such trumpery moonshine in my life. All this ridiculous, SELBANEV POPILLOL nonsense – I...

VENABLES: Oh, but, sir, I *did* pay it back. Jennings has forgotten to cross it off, sir.

MR. WILKINS: Be quiet, Selbanev – er, I mean Venables. We're in the middle of a maths test. This is no time to start bothering about your wretched popillols – er, lillypips...

VENABLES: Lollipops, sir.

MR. WILKINS: That's what I said. Now look here, Jennings, I... Oh! This is the piece you were writing when I called you up, was it?

JENNINGS: Yes, sir.

MR. WILKINS: *Very* interesting, I'm sure! Unfortunately for you, Jennings, I can work out this for myself. "RETSIM SNIKLIW: G-NISSIM K-NIL". That, you impudent little boy, means: "Mr. Wilkins – Missing Link!"

Laughter reaction

JENNINGS: Yes, that's right, sir. I thought...

MR. WILKINS: How dare you say I'm the missing link?

JENNINGS: Oh, but I didn't, sir.

MR. WILKINS: Don't try to deny it. You put in your diary that I belong to a sub-human anthropoidal species, and what's more you wrote it in code and tried to make a secret of it. Well, I won't have it kept a secret!

JENNINGS: There's no secret about it, really sir. Lots of people know; those who understand the code, that is. But you don't understand, sir, what I really mean...

MR. WILKINS: I understand perfectly well, Jennings. I shall confiscate this diary till the end of the term.

JENNINGS: Oh, but sir, please! I've promised my Aunt Angela to write something in it every day without fail, sir.

MR. WILKINS: You shouldn't make these rash promises.

JENNINGS: She'll be terribly disappointed, sir – and well, I was wondering whether…

MR. WILKINS: I'm confiscating this diary – I've just said so.

JENNINGS: Oh yes, I know, sir. But would you, just for Aunt Angela's sake – would you agree to *lend* it back to me for about two minutes every evening, so's I can keep it up to date sir?

MR. WILKINS: Well, I… I… Queer sort of confiscation, I must say!

JENNINGS: Oh, please, sir; it's terribly important. I'll work ever so hard to make up for it, sir.

MR. WILKINS: Let me see you doing it, first. You get all the rest of these sums right and I'll see about letting you write your diary up when you go to bed.

JENNINGS: Thank you, sir.

MR. WILKINS: But only on loan, mind! Now sit down… Next sum. "If a hen and a half lays an egg and a half in a – er, no, that's wrong. If a hen lays an egg…"

Fade out / music / fade in

JENNINGS: (*calling*) Darbishire… Darbishire! I say, Venables, have you seen Darbishire? It's urgent.

VENABLES: Yes, he went along here a moment ago, Jennings. What d'you want him for?

JENNINGS: Something ghastly's happened. Help me to find him.

VENABLES: Let's have a squint in the common room.

They go, ad lib / Fade up common room background

Yes, there he is. Hey, Darbishire, Jennings wants you.

DARBISHIRE: Why, what's up?

JENNINGS: Listen, Darbi, I've made the most supersonic bish. You know I got all those sums right, and Old Wilkie said I could borrow my diary back just for when I went to bed every night?

DARBISHIRE: Yes.

JENNINGS: Well, he gave it to me in the dorm the night before last, and I wrote it up and promised to give it back to him in the morning.

DARBISHIRE: Well?

JENNINGS: I forgot; and he didn't ask me for it. And now I've lost the thing.

DARBISHIRE: How did you come to do that?

JENNINGS: I don't know. It's just vanished – like his cuff-link.

I've looked everywhere. I just daren't face Wilkie again till I've found it.

DARBISHIRE: I wonder if it dropped out of your pocket when Mr. Carter took us for that walk yesterday afternoon.

JENNINGS: Golly, yes – I never thought! I bet that's what happened. I was charging about quite a lot when he let us break line on the meadow.

VENABLES: Well in that case, it's no good looking round the school for it. It might be anywhere. You'd better ask at the police station if anyone's handed it in.

DARBISHIRE: Perhaps Mr. Carter would let you telephone as it's urgent.

JENNINGS: I can't do that. I don't know the number.

DARBISHIRE: You could easily find out. Ring them up and ask them.

JENNINGS: Don't be such a prehistoric remains, Darbi. If I could do that I wouldn't need to ask them. No, I'd rather go to the police station and *see* them: it's a wizard sight too difficult to explain over the phone.

VENABLES: I don't see anything hard about asking if someone's handed in a diary.

JENNINGS: But don't you see, Venables, if the police have got hold of it, I'll have to go and explain things to them. All those names in code, for instance. – SELBANEV and NOSNIKTA and RETSIM RETRAC and Co – the police may think they're foreign agents and things.

VENABLES: Oh, don't be crazy!

JENNINGS: Well, Mr. Carter said they sounded like members of an Eastern European spy organisation to him – and *he* ought to know.

DARBISHIRE: Phew! Did Mr. Carter really say that?

JENNINGS: Yes. And where it's written partly in code and partly in English it looks even more suspicious. There's things like "RETSIM SNIKLIW exploded atom bomb, today."

VENABLES: Gosh, what's that mean?

JENNINGS: Well, it was just a way of saying that Mr. Wilkins got into a bate and shouted at me, but it sounds sinister, doesn't it? And then there's bits like, "RETSIM RETRAC discovered secret plans of YROTIMROD DEEF" when Mr. Carter found out we were planning to have a feed in the dormitory. I wrote it half-and-half like that specially so's the

79

masters wouldn't know what it meant, but whatever are the police going to think!

DARBISHIRE: Yes, it's just the sort of thing that any decent spy *would* write in his diary. I should go and tell Mr. Carter if I were you, Jen.

VENABLES: I shouldn't! I'd have a bash at getting it back from the police first. There'll be an awful hoo-hah if the Head wakes up and finds Scotland Yard all over the football pitch, looking for SELBANEV and RETSIM RETRAC and the atom bomb plans.

JENNINGS: I think you're right, Venables... Come with me Darbi?

DARBISHIRE: I suppose I'd better. After all, if it ever leaks out in official circles that ERIH-SIBRAD is really me, spelt in reverse gear, it'll take a bit of explaining, won't it!

JENNINGS: I vote we borrow bikes and go now.

DARBISHIRE: Righto. Temple will lend me his if I put him on my cake list.

VENABLES: You can borrow mine, if you like, Jen.

JENNINGS: Thanks, Venables.

VENABLES: It's got a slow puncture in the back tyre, but it'll be all right if you pump it up again for the return journey.

JENNINGS: Okay. Come on then, Darbi... Oh, heavens, I hope the police haven't started the spy-hunt already...

Fade out/fade in

ATKINSON: Venables! Oh, there you are, Venables. I've been looking for you everywhere.

VENABLES: Hullo, Atkinson. What d'you want me for?

ATKINSON: Do you mind if I borrow your bicycle pump?

VENABLES: Sorry; I've lent it to Jennings. He and Darbishire have just this minute beetled off on a super important mission.

ATKINSON: Oh! Well, they've gone without the pump, then. Here it is, look. I took it off your bike ten minutes ago.

VENABLES: Well, I like the cheek of that, Atkinson! You never asked if you could borrow it.

ATKINSON: I'm asking you now. You weren't about when I wanted it and, anyway, I had to pump my tyres up – I've had permish to go for a ride.

VENABLES: Well you can jolly well ride after Jennings and give him the pump back. He doesn't know he's gone without it and he's got a slow puncture.

ATKINSON: Okay; I will, if I see him in the village, but I can't hang about; I'm going on to Dunhambury.

VENABLES: You'll find my bike outside the police station.

ATKINSON: Police station! Golly! Whatever's...?

VENABLES: Oh, it's all right. Jennings is just making a few private enquiries. If he's gone in when you get there, leave the pump where he'll see it when he comes out. Don't put it on the bike, though – the bracket's a bit wobbly. I'd rather he carried it.

ATKINSON: I won't forget. But what's he really gone to the police about?

VENABLES: Suspected espionage, but don't tell anyone.

ATKINSON: Phew! You mean Jennings thinks he's found a spy?

VENABLES: No; he's afraid the police will think *he's* one. It looks pretty black against him, on paper, but there's just a chance he'll be able to clear himself before Scotland Yard start pouncing.

ATKINSON: Gosh, how *wizard*! – I mean, poor old Jennings. Is there anything I can do to help him?

VENABLES: Yes, there is. You can take my pump along and leave it where he's sure to find it when he comes out...

Fade out/fade in. Bicycle bell

DARBISHIRE: Phew! Not so fast, Jennings. I can't ride uphill at 90 miles an hour.

JENNINGS: We can't afford to waste time, Darbi. What with Old Wilkie and Aunt Angela and now the police all wanting to know about my diary, there isn't a moment to lose... Here we are; that's where the village policeman lives – that house with "Constabulary" over the front door. Lean the bikes up outside the gate and we'll get cracking.

Dismounting and parking of bicycles

DARBISHIRE: You know, Jen, I don't like getting mixed up in criminal proceedings and things.

JENNINGS: Oh, don't talk such antiseptic eyewash, Darbi. It's just a straightforward matter about a lost diary – at least I hope so.

DARBISHIRE: My father says that if once you get on the wrong side of the law...

JENNINGS: Leave your father out of this, for heaven's sake! I've got enough on my mind as it is.

DARBISHIRE: But there's no knowing what'll happen. They may even want to take your fingerprints. Is that why you're taking your gloves off, all ready?

JENNINGS: No, it isn't! And for goodness sake don't get so windy. Your job is to keep me cool and calm and...

DARBISHIRE: Heavens, Jen, that's torn it! You've left them on the gate!

JENNINGS: What – my gloves?

DARBISHIRE: No, your fingerprints.

JENNINGS: Don't be so stark, raving bats! You're giving me the jitters, now. Come along in. (*Footsteps on path.*) The front door's open, let's go and see...

DARBISHIRE: Do you think we really ought to?

JENNINGS: What do you think we've come all this way for? There's a bell in the passage, just by that little hatch.

DARBISHIRE: Bags you ring it, then.

JENNINGS: Of course I will! I've got nothing to hide. Here we go.

Bell rings

I shall just tell him straight out what the code really means and...

Hatch opens

POLICEMAN: Yes, sonny – what can I do for you?

JENNINGS: I wish to speak to a policeman, please.

POLICEMAN: Your wish is granted, sonny. I *am* a policeman.

JENNINGS: Er, yes. Has anyone given you a diary, lately?

POLICEMAN: As a present, do you mean? Or handed in as lost property?

JENNINGS: Lost property. You see mine's gone, and what I want to explain is that if anyone brings it to you, all that stuff about SELBANEV and NOSNIKTA and RETSIM RETRAC – well, it doesn't mean what you think it means.

POLICEMAN: Oh, no? And what am I *supposed* to think it means?

JENNINGS: The Eastern Europe Spy Organisation, of course. You see the diary says things like RETSIM SNIKLIW exploded an atom bomb last Thursday.

POLICEMAN: Dear me!... And didn't he?

JENNINGS: No, not really. And all that about RETSIM RETRAC discovering the secret plans – well, you'd laugh if you knew what they really were. (*Laughs uneasily*) Just a few doughnuts after lights out, that's all. (*Laughs again*

82

uneasily)

POLICEMAN: Now look: let's get this straight. You've come to report the loss of a diary?

JENNINGS: Yes, but...

POLICEMAN: Right. Now, what's your name?

JENNINGS: Well, strictly speaking, it's Jennings; but in code, of course, it's S-G-NINNEJ.

DARBISHIRE: It's the same with me. You'll find I'm ERIH-SIBRAD, backwards.

POLICEMAN: I'll find *what* is ERIH-SIBRAD, backwards?

JENNINGS: The name. And the address, too. YRUBNIL TRU-OC YROT-ARA-PERP LOOHCS.

POLICEMAN: Are you trying to tell me that's where you live?

JENNINGS: Oh no; not really of course.

DARBISHIRE: Be careful, Jen. It's a criminal offence to give the police a false address.

JENNINGS: Oh, but I'm not: my address in Linbury Court School.

POLICEMAN: You said something quite different a moment ago.

JENNINGS: Yes, but don't you see...

POLICEMAN: Now look here, sonny – you've lost your diary; all right, I'll make a note of it, but I've no time for fun and games. Run along and try your jokes on somebody else. Good morning.

Hatch slams shut

JENNINGS: Well!

DARBISHIRE: You are an ass, Jen. You made the most frightful bish of the whole issue. I'm sure he didn't understand what you were talking about.

JENNINGS: I was a bit worked up, that's why. Still, he can't suspect me of being mixed up with the spies now I've told him everything. Now we'd better... Darbi! Look, someone's left their bicycle pump on the wall – bang outside the police station, too. That was careless of them. I'd better hand it in: the same as I'd expect anyone to do if they found my diary.

DARBISHIRE: (*going*) All right. But don't be long. I'll wait here for you.

JENNINGS: All right.

Pause. Bell: Pause: Hatch opens

POLICEMAN: Now look here: I thought I told you to run away.

JENNINGS: Yes, but I've come to report something I've found – not something I've lost. It's this pump: I thought I ought to bring it in.

POLICEMAN: All right, I'll book it down... What did you say your name was?

JENNINGS: Well, my real name's Jennings, but according to the code it's – well, it's rather difficult to pronounce. Try saying...

POLICEMAN: That'll do; I've had enough of this nonsense. If your name's Jennings...

DARBISHIRE: (*approaching*) Sir!... I mean Constable...

POLICEMAN: Well, what do you want?

DARBISHIRE: Oh, excuse me, sir... I mean Constable, but you know that bicycle pump my friend just brought in?

POLICEMAN: Yes?

DARBISHIRE: Well, I was wondering whether you'd very kindly let him have it back.

POLICEMAN: If it's not claimed in three months I'll send him a postcard.

JENNINGS: Oh, thank you.

DARBISHIRE: Oh, but it is claimed; he's claiming it now. It's the pump off your bike, Jennings.

POLICEMAN: Talk sense; it can't be his. He's just brought it in as lost property.

DARBISHIRE: He's made a sort of accidental bish, that's all. I've just found out, Jen; Atkinson just rode up on his bike to see whether we'd got it all right.

JENNINGS: Well, fancy that! I'll have to claim it at once, won't I? I'm sorry about this. It's the sort of mistake that could happen to anyone.

POLICEMAN: Is it? There's not many as bring their own possessions in here as lost property and then claim them half a minute later.

JENNINGS: Oh, but it isn't mine really.

POLICEMAN: Not yours. Cor! Stone the crows. You just said it was!

JENNINGS: Well, actually it belongs to a chap called Venables, but in the diary his name's SELBANEV, of course.

POLICEMAN: (*sarcastically*) Oh, of course – it would be!

JENNINGS: Yes, SELBANEV is backwards you see – like

RETSIM SNIKLIW – the one who exploded the atom bomb; only he didn't, really, of course.

POLICEMAN: You're quite sure he hasn't lost his pump too?

JENNINGS: No, he's only got a link missing.

POLICEMAN: Not the only one, I'd say.

JENNINGS: But it was all his fault, really, about the diary, because I was writing it up in bed and he came in to put the light out and... Darbi! I've just remembered where I left it!

DARBISHIRE: Where?

JENNINGS: In my pyjamas. I bunged it in the pocket when the light went out and I forgot about it next morning. Oh, wizzo, that makes everything all right. You needn't worry about it being lost any more.

DARBISHIRE: Yes, that'll be a weight off your mind, won't it? And thank you so much for helping us to find it sir... I mean Constable. I do hope we haven't been wasting your time.

POLICEMAN: Oh, not at all. Not at all. You come here blathering about atom bombs and secret plans and foreign spies with unpronounceable names – and on top of that you don't know whether your own property ought to be lost or claimed or even whether it *is* your property at all! Here, take your pump and go and blow up your atom bombs with it! I've had enough.

Hatch slams shut. Music / fade in

JENNINGS: (*calling*) Matron, please Matron, may I go into the dormitory and get my pyjamas?

MATRON: Going to bed already, Jennings?

JENNINGS: No, Matron, but I've left my diary in the pocket. Darbishire and I have just ridden all the way back from the village in seven minutes to get it, haven't we, Darbi?

DARBISHIRE: Yes, I don't know how many long-distance cycling records we haven't smashed.

MATRON: I'm afraid you're too late. Your pyjamas won't be in your dormitory; I packed them to go to the laundry this morning.

DARBISHIRE: Laundry! Oh, fish-hooks, and after all the trouble we've been to. It'll be ruined when it comes back. Either it'll be so starched you can't turn the pages over, or it'll be so mangled you can't read them.

MATRON: I don't think the laundry man's called yet. If you look of the landing you may find the baskets are still there, but be

85

careful not to make a mess. Put everything back exactly as you find it.

JENNINGS: Yes, of course, Matron. Come on, Darbi.

Door opens

There they are: just at the end of the passage. Socko!... What a lot of baskets – I wonder which one's ours? They're all labelled. Dorm 6 – that's no good... Dorm 3... Here we are: Dormitory 4 and Staff. Help me lift it down.

Bumping of basket, lid opens

They should be here somewhere. Golly, what a clutter – shirts, socks, towels, handkerchiefs. We'll have to chuck them all . out: the pyjamas are at the bottom, I expect.

DARBISHIRE: There they are – red and white stripes.

JENNINGS: Let me get at them then... Hooray! Super-socko-sonic. Here's my diary in the pocket!

DARBISHIRE: Jolly good – hooray! Hooray!

JENNINGS: We'd better put all the dirty washing back now. Help me bundle it in.

DARBISHIRE: Righto. We shall have to squash it a bit tighter though or it won't go back. I'll pass the things to you, and you squash. Here's my last week's vest – fancy seeing that again! Put it back carefully... Atkinson's dirty towel... and here's a large white shirt – must be a master's.

JENNINGS: Yes, it's Old Wilkie's. He was wearing one like this last – Oh, gosh, Darbi! What do you think I've found?

DARBISHIRE: What?

JENNINGS: Mr. Wilkins' missing cuff-link.

DARBISHIRE: No!

JENNINGS: Yes. Slap-bang-doyng in the cuff of his shirt. He must have bunged it in the basket without taking it out.

DARBISHIRE: I say, he will be pleased. This old basket's quite a treasure trove, one way and another. First we solve the mystery of the secret diary and now the riddle of the missing link. I wonder what we'll stumble across next?

JENNINGS: Mr. Wilkins, I should think. He's coming up the stairs now. He can't grumble at us this time, considering what we've found for him.

DARBISHIRE: No, but I expect we'll have a good try.

MR. WILKINS: (*approaching*) What on earth are you two boys doing up here on the landing? You're supposed to be... Good gracious! Just look at this washing basket – laundry strewn about like autumn leaves.

JENNINGS: Oh, but, sir, Matron said we...

MR. WILKINS: I'm quite sure she said nothing of the kind... oh, yes, Jennings, that reminds me – I gave you your diary back on the distinct understanding that it was to be returned to me as soon as you'd written up the day's entries.

JENNINGS: I meant to give it to you before, but I lost it, sir.

MR. WILKINS: Lost it! Gross carelessness, as usual.

JENNINGS: I've got it back now, sir, and I went to an awful lot of trouble so it wouldn't get into the wrong hands. Here it is, sir.

MR. WILKINS: And another time I... here, what's this inside the cover? My cuff-link – the one I lost.

JENNINGS: Yes sir, we found it mixed up with the laundry.

MR. WILKINS: That was very clever of you, Jennings. Very clever indeed. Thanks very much. I'm more than grateful to get this back again.

JENNINGS: That's all right, sir.

DARBISHIRE: Of course, if we hadn't been looking for Jennings' diary we shouldn't have found it, sir.

MR. WILKINS: Oh, really! Well, in that case the fairest thing I can do is to give you your diary back in exchange, Jennings.

JENNINGS: Oh, thank you so much, sir. Aunt Angela will be pleased.

MR. WILKINS: But no more funny descriptions of me, mind.

JENNINGS: Oh, but I never did that, sir. All that about you and the missing link was to remind me to...

MR. WILKINS: Why, of course – how stupid of me! I'd forgotten you said you were going to make a note of it. And there I was thinking – ha – ha - ha! (*going*) I must go and tell Matron. She'll be tickled pink...

DARBISHIRE: Well, come on, Jen: don't stand there reading your diary and leave me all the tidying up to do.

JENNINGS: I was just thinking what to write in it this evening. You see Mr. Carter was on at me to write really first-class interesting stuff like Samuel Pepys and Mrs. Dale and all that lot.

DARBISHIRE: I expect you'll think of something. After all, I bet Mrs. Dale never got mixed up in a supersonic hoo-hah with the police like you did.

JENNINGS: That's what I mean. It's got to be something really decent to show Mr. Carter tonight.

Cross fade to dormitory background

MR. CARTER: Hurry up, Jennings. You're not nearly undressed and you've been sitting on your bed chewing that pencil for the last ten minutes.

JENNINGS: Yes, sir. I was just doing my diary specially for you to see, sir.

MR. CARTER: You've plenty of material today. Darbishire was telling me at tea time of the most amazing discoveries, all mixed up with bicycle pumps, incredulous policemen and European spy rings. It should be well worth reading.

JENNINGS: Yes, sir. Would you like to see what I've put. Here it is, sir.

MR. CARTER: Thank you. According to Darbishire you could have written a three-act play about... Oh, Jennings! Is this really the best you can do? "Fairly warm toddy. Sorted washing."

JENNINGS: I couldn't think of anything else to put, sir.

MR. CARTER: Oh, dear, oh, dear! Well, all I can say is that if your generous Aunt Angela is willing to part with five shillings for a feeble description like that, however much would she pay if she knew the whole story? "Fairly warm toddy. Sorted washing." Fairly warm toddy...

Music.

Linbury Court Preparatory School

Dear David,

I would not tell everybody this, but I don't
mind you knowing if you will not spread it,
except to chaps you can trust. Last week
Darbishire and I had a pet secret which was
really a secret pet, and as it was not allowed we
had to keep it quiet. This is not meant for a
joke, it is serious, as you will see when I say
that our pet guinea pig was the same one as Mr
Wilkins' pet aversion - although it was neither
of us's property, really. If this sounds
mysterious it is because of our guinea pig being
on the secret list like new jet-fighters and
things. I must stop now owing to blotch famine,
but will tell you all about it on Wed.
Yours affeckly,

J.C.T. Jennings.

JENNINGS
AND THE SECRET PET

(Fourth series no.5)

Jennings and the Secret Pet was the twenty-fifth Jennings play.

It was first broadcast by the BBC Home Service for Children's Hour on Wednesday 30th January 1952 with the following cast:

JENNINGS	John Charlesworth
DARBISHIRE	Henry Searle
MR. CARTER	Geoffrey Wincott
MR. WILKINS	Wilfred Babbage

Produced by David Davis

Fade in door knocks (off)

MR. WILKINS: Yes?... Come in!

Pause. Door knocks repeated

(*irritably*) Oh, come in, come in, if you want to. Don't stand outside beating the door panels like a – like a panel beater. Come in!

Door opens

Well, what is it now?... Oh, I beg your pardon, Carter. I didn't know it was you – thought it was one of the boys.

MR. CARTER: That's all right, Wilkins. I just looked in to... I say, what on earth are you doing under the table – inspecting the floor boards for dry rot?

MR. WILKINS: (*off*) No, no, nothing like that.

MR. CARTER: Then why crawl around the room on all fours?

MR. WILKINS: (*off*) I'm looking for something, but I'm afraid I'm too late.

MR. CARTER: And what have you lost this time, Wilkins?

MR. WILKINS: (*approach*) As a matter of fact, Carter, I'm looking for – well, I know it sounds a little improbable, but between you and me, I've lost a guinea-pig.

MR. CARTER: A guinea-pig! I never knew you kept guinea-pigs, Wilkins.

MR. WILKINS: I don't keep guinea-pigs. I wouldn't keep them for a fortune. This wretched animal doesn't belong to me.

MR. CARTER: Well, it doesn't belong to one of the boys, surely! The headmaster stopped them keeping pets after Jennings took that goldfish for a dip in the swimming bath, you remember.

MR. WILKINS: I know – that's why I'm in charge of this one. Or why I *was* in charge, I should say. It's all the fault of that wretched boy, Atkinson, being whisked off to the sick room with a sprained ankle.

MR. CARTER: I don't follow: why does that make you guardian to a guinea-pig?

MR. WILKINS: The boy's grandmother came to see him yesterday and, well, you know what these doting grandmothers are. She thought he'd like a pet to cheer him up so she arrived at the sick room complete with a guinea-pig in a box.

MR. CARTER: I should have thought Matron would have explained that pets were against the rules.

MR. WILKINS: Matron was out – that was the trouble. And when she got back, Grandmother Atkinson had gone home and left this wretched rodent behind. I tell you, Carter, some of these old ladies have got just no idea of school rules. The headmaster asked me to take charge of the thing and ring her up and ask her to come back and collect it.

MR. CARTER: And have you done so?

MR. WILKINS: Yes: she's coming this afternoon. And now the beastly animal's escaped. I left it here in the box during lunch, and when I came back – well, you can see for yourself. It's hopped over the side and gone to earth somewhere.

MR. CARTER: Are you sure the door was closed when you went down to lunch?

MR. WILKINS: Oh! I hadn't thought of that. Yes, I believe I did leave it ajar now you come to mention it. You know, Carter, some of these animals are as bad as the grandmothers. As soon as you take your eye off them...

MR. CARTER: I should look a bit further afield, if I were you.

MR. WILKINS: Yes, I will. And I'd better get hold of some cabbage leaves or something to feed it on when I find it.

MR. CARTER: *If* you find it. Atkinson's grandmother won't be very pleased if she comes all this way to collect it and then finds you've brought her on a wild goose chase.

MR. WILKINS: I know, I know! Don't talk to me about wild goose chases. Let's get the wild guinea-pig chase over first. I tell you, Carter, I'm just about fed up with the whole business. My job's looking after boys, not looking after livestock, and if people like Atkinson's grandmother had their way, I might just as well buy myself a shiny peaked cap and get a job at the zoo.

MR. CARTER: *(chuckles)* Well, good hunting, Wilkins. If I meet you trailing a cabbage along on a piece of string, I shall know it's all in a good cause.

MR. WILKINS: Very funny, I'm sure. *(fading)* Well, I'll go and start my small game hunt in the classrooms and work down to the boot-room.

Music. Fade in

DARBISHIRE: *(calling)* Jennings... Jennings! Oh, there you are, Jen. Whatever are you doing skulking down here in the boot-room? I've been looking all over for you.

93

JENNINGS: Ssh! Don't make such a cracking row, Darbishire. You'll have everyone coming down to see what's going on.

DARBISHIRE: Well, what *is* going on?

JENNINGS: Ssh! I've made a supersonic discovery, but it's a top priority secret. I've discovered an animal.

DARBISHIRE: Discovered an animal! What, you mean a new rare species that no one ever knew about before?

JENNINGS: Oh, no; it's only rare in places where you're not allowed to keep pets. I'll show you. I've put him in the waste-paper basket for safety.

DARBISHIRE: Gosh, that doesn't sound very safe. They emptied it three times last term.

JENNINGS: It's only for the time being – here he is, look: isn't he super?

DARBISHIRE: Golly – a guinea-pig! How wizzo-cracking-sonic.

JENNINGS: Ssh! Don't broadcast it like that. There'd be an awful hoo-hah if Mr. Wilkins or anyone knew there was a guinea-pig on the premises.

DARBISHIRE: Yes, of course. But wherever did you get it from?

JENNINGS: I found him, just after lunch. I was hoofing along to the boot-room to look for that house shoe I lost, and there it was.

DARBISHIRE: The house shoe?

JENNINGS: No, you coot – the guinea-pig.

DARBISHIRE: I say, isn't he socko! I wonder who he belongs to?

JENNINGS: That's the mystery. He can't possibly belong to any of the chaps in this school, because we don't have pets.

DARBISHIRE: Well, it must belong to someone – Matron, perhaps.

JENNINGS: Heavens, no; she's got a cat. A guinea-pig wouldn't go down well with a cat, at all.

DARBISHIRE: It might go down *too* well. It's a bit of a puzzle, all right.

JENNINGS: I know. And we can't take him to a master or there'd be a hoo-hah, so I vote we keep him till we know who it belongs to. First of all, though, we ought to get him something to eat.

DARBISHIRE: I wonder if he'd like a chunk of apple? (*going to look*) I left quite a decent core in my boot-locker when the lunch bell went. It'll be just the... well, that's funny – it's gone! (*coming back*) Now who's eaten my apple core, I'd like to know.

JENNINGS: It could have been lots of people.

DARBISHIRE: Well, if lots of people *did* eat it, they wouldn't have got much each. It wasn't all that big.

JENNINGS: No, I mean it could have been anyone. Me, for instance – only it wasn't.

DARBISHIRE: Or even me. Gosh, yes, I remember now, it *was* me. I came back and polished it off because I remembered there was only cabbage for lunch... and I always leave mine, unless Matron's watching.

JENNINGS: Well, never mind. We'll go and find something. I vote we leave him in the waste-paper basket for now; he can't get out and no one's likely to look inside.

DARBISHIRE: And he's got quite a decent view of the boot-lockers, too. Come on then, Jennings, let's have a squint outside the kitchen door. We might find the remains of my cabbage in the pig food bin.

JENNINGS: Righto.

Fade out / fade in

I say, it's super exciting having a secret pet, isn't it?

DARBISHIRE: I know. What are you going to call him?

JENNINGS: I think I'll call him F. J. Saunders.

DARBISHIRE: Why?

JENNINGS: Well, why not? Why are you called Darbishire?

DARBISHIRE: Oh, that's easy. My father says that years ago our family used to be known as D apostrophe Arbi, D'Arbi...

JENNINGS: All right, all right – we haven't got time now for the story of your life. We've got to concentrate on what we're doing in case we meet Mr. Carter or someone. Besides, he looks just like a man I know at home.

DARBISHIRE: Who does – Mr. Carter?

JENNINGS: No, you crumbling ruin; the guinea-pig looks like this chap I was telling you about – F. J. Saunders. At least, that's what *I* call him: in fact, everybody does. Why, even the vicar calls him Mr. Saunders.

DARBISHIRE: Does he – why?

JENNINGS: Because it's his name. Honestly, Darbi, you do ask the most cootish questions. Anyone would think you were stark raving crackers to listen to...

DARBISHIRE: I say, cave, Jennings. There's Mr. Wilkins going down the corridor. He's just going round the bend.

JENNINGS: Well, what of it? It's a free country. Anyway, *you* can't talk about people going round the bend when you ask such crazy questions about whether...

DARBISHIRE: No, I meant Old Wilkie's hoofing towards the basement. Don't you think we ought to head him away from the boot-room till we've got F. J. Saunders in a safe place? We don't want him rummaging about in the waste-paper basket, do we?

JENNINGS: Don't be so windy, Darbi. Why on earth should he? You only do that sort of thing if you've lost something. Come along let's go through here; it'll bring us out by the kitchen.

Fade out / Fade in

Here we are. And there's the pig-food bin, outside the kitchen door.

DARBISHIRE: Golly, yes – and just stuffed to bursting with outside cabbage leaves. D'you think it would be all right to help ourselves?

JENNINGS: I don't see why not. After all, F. J. Saunders is a *sort* of pig isn't he?

DARBISHIRE: M'yes, in a way. All the same, I'd feel happier if they'd painted "guinea" on the lid as well as "pig food".

JENNINGS: Let's fill our pockets and then go and give Saunders a really first class one-course dinner.

DARBISHIRE: Righto, then.

Ad lib they root: then: bin lid dropped

JENNINGS: That's got it.

DARBISHIRE: Good job guinea-pigs like their cabbage raw, isn't it?

JENNINGS: I don't think they're fussy whether it's cooked or not.

DARBISHIRE: I was thinking of our pockets. I'm not what you'd call fussy, either, but Matron would have something to say if we went about with pocketfuls of steaming greens... There, I've filled mine – no one'll spot it if I pull my pocket flaps well down.

JENNINGS: Okay, we've got enough now. We'll go back the way we came, and after Saunders has had his dinner we'll make him a hutch.

DARBISHIRE: Yes, but we can't keep it in the boot-room. If the masters see us beetling down to the lockers every feeding-time, they may small a rat.

JENNINGS: Why should they?

DARBISHIRE: Well, they might smell a guinea-pig, then. That'd put the cat among the pigeons, wouldn't it?

JENNINGS: Don't talk such antiseptic eyewash, Darbishire. There's nothing to worry about so long as we're careful and don't start bringing cats and pigeons in as well. And then at the end of the term... Oh, I say, look out! Here comes Mr. Carter: try and look natural.

DARBISHIRE: I never can look natural when I try to.

JENNINGS: Ssh!

MR. CARTER: (approaching) Hullo, where have you two been?

JENNINGS: We – er, we've just been for a stroll round the kitchen yard, sir.

MR. CARTER: I see. Round the kitchen yard.

JENNINGS: Yes, sir.

MR. CARTER: Just a quiet stroll, eh?.

JENNINGS: Yes, sir.

MR. CARTER: But you're supposed to be in the common-room and... Oh, really, Jennings – just look at your pockets. I've told you a dozen times not to fill them to bursting point with useless junk.   .

JENNINGS: No, sir.

MR. CARTER: And your pockets are just as bad, Darbishire.

DARBISHIRE: Yes, sir.

MR. CARTER: Whatever have you got in them?

DARBISHIRE: Er – cabbage, sir.

MR. CARTER: Cabbage! But, good heavens boy, why?

DARBISHIRE: Oh, it's quite all right, sir – it isn't cooked, or anything.

MR. CARTER: I should hope not indeed. But why on earth...? Are you cabbage-laden as well, Jennings?

JENNINGS: Yes, sir. Well actually, the point is, as you might say, we found these cabbage leaves, you see, sir...

MR. CARTER: No, Jennings, I don't see. In fact the whole thing... Wait! Light is beginning to dawn. Have you just seen Mr. Wilkins?

JENNINGS: Yes, sir; just a few minutes ago, sir.

MR. CARTER: Ah, that explains it. He did say something about cabbage-collecting, now I come to think of it. You'd better run along and find him: I expect he's waiting for it.

JENNINGS: Yes, sir. Er – take the cabbage to Mr. Wilkins, do you mean, sir?

MR. CARTER: Well, of course! You're not proposing to eat it yourself, are you?

JENNINGS: Oh, no, sir.

MR. CARTER: (*fading*) That's all right, then. But you needn't carry it in your pockets. That won't improve your suit, or the cabbage either.

JENNINGS: No, sir... Well, whatever do you make of that, Darbi? Fancy, Old Wilkie wanting raw cabbage! I'd never noticed he was a vegetarian.

DARBISHIRE: And just after lunch, too; it doesn't make sense. However hungry he is you'd think he'd draw the line at the outside leaves, wouldn't you?

JENNINGS: Yes; besides it won't be fair to F. J. Saunders if we give his dinner to Mr. Wilkins. You are a prehistoric bazooka, Darbishire, letting Mr. Carter see your pockets bulging like that. We could have kept the whole lot otherwise.

DARBISHIRE: Well, I like that! Your pockets were just as bulgy, so you can't talk. You're like those people my father talks about who live in glass houses and can't throw stones.

JENNINGS: Why can't they? And what's throwing stones got to do with pocketfuls of cabbage? I don't live in a glass house, anyway.

DARBISHIRE: No, I didn't really mean *you* did. It was just a saying. There are no such things as glass houses, really.

JENNINGS: There wizard well are! My uncle's got one: he grows tomatoes in it, so that proves it!

DARBISHIRE: Yes, I know, but I was talking about the other sort.

JENNINGS: What other sort?

DARBISHIRE: The sort that if you live in them you shouldn't throw stones.

JENNINGS: But a moment ago you said there *was* no other sort. You told me there was no such thing.

DARBISHIRE: Ah, but I meant – well, never mind. I say, there's Old Wilkie now, just coming out of his room. We'd better go and offer him some cabbage, hadn't we?

JENNINGS: Don't be crazy, Darbi. He won't take it, *really*. Mr. Carter was just pulling our legs. After all, Old Wilkie is *human* – more or less.

DARBISHIRE: Well, Mr. Carter *did* say.

JENNINGS: All right, then – you offer him some and see. I bet you a million pounds he blows up and ticks you off for trying to be funny. Go on – I dare you to.

DARBISHIRE: All right, I will. I shall put the blame on Mr. Carter if he does. Masters shouldn't make jokes that lead to... oh, sir, Mr. Wilkins, sir!

MR. WILKINS: *(approaching)* Yes, what is it, Darbishire?

DARBISHIRE: Sir, would you like... oh, no, it's all right, sir. It doesn't matter.

MR. WILKINS: Go on, boy, go on. Would I like what?

DARBISHIRE: Well, it was just something that Mr. Carter said, but perhaps he didn't mean it, of course, or he wouldn't have said it. I mean, well – he told me to ask you if you'd like some raw cabbage, sir.

MR. WILKINS: Yes, I certainly should, Darbishire. Just what I wanted; and you couldn't have brought it at a more opportune moment. Thank you, Darbishire, I'll take it into my room straight away. *(going)* Most opportune. Couldn't have been better...

Door shuts: off

DARBISHIRE: There you are, Jennings. What did I tell you?

JENNINGS: Well! Gosh! What do you know! Things have come to a fine state when masters shut themselves up in their rooms and eat raw cabbage leaves, slap-bang-doyng on top of their lunch.

DARBISHIRE: It's amazing, isn't it? Still, my father says there's no accounting for taste. Not that there's much taste to account for in raw cabbage, of course.

JENNINGS: Come along. I've still got my load intact for F. J. Saunders. We'd better hurry up and feed him before Old Wilkie pounces like a swarm of locusts and gobbles up all the vegetation for miles around.

Fade out/in

DARBISHIRE: Here we are – good old boot-room!

JENNINGS: Wait a minute, Darbi, *(going)* while I get the waste-paper basket and see if he's... oh, heavens! Golly, Darbishire!

DARBISHIRE: What's the matter?

JENNINGS: (*Coming back*) He's gone!

DARBISHIRE: What?

JENNINGS: Yes, the basket's empty. He's escaped.

DARBISHIRE: Oh, fish-hooks!

JENNINGS: He's not anywhere in the boot-room – you can see: there aren't even any footprints or paw marks or anything. I reckon he must have run along the top of the boot-lockers and beetled out through the bottom of the window. In that case he'll be somewhere in the head's garden by now.

DARBISHIRE: Oh, heavens; we can't go there; it's out of bounds.

JENNINGS: We'll have to risk it, that's all. Faint heart never won fair guinea-pig or whatever it was. It should be all right anyway, because I saw the head go out in his car directly after lunch. So now's our chance.

DARBISHIRE: Righto, then! We'll strike, willy-nilly, while the iron is hot, as my father says.

JENNINGS: I'm not striking anyone with hot irons, whatever your father says. Besides I wouldn't know this Willy character if I met him.

DARBISHIRE: You don't understand. There's no such person as Willy-nilly, really. It means *will*-ye *nill*-ye, that means...

JENNINGS: Yes, I daresay, but we've got to get on the trail right away. You know, it really is the rottenest hunk of bad luck. I was beginning to get really fond of F. J. Saunders, and now this has to happen.

DARBISHIRE: It's always the way, isn't it? Why do these ghastly catastroscopes always have to pick on us to happen to!

Fade out/fade in – door opens

MR. WILKINS: Are, there you are, Carter; I thought I'd find you in the staff room. I say, what do you think? I've found it.

MR. CARTER: Found what, Wilkins?

MR. WILKINS: That wretched guinea-pig, of course. Quite by chance, too. I was looking round in the boot-room and I heard a funny sort of noise in the waste-paper basket. Scrritch – scrratch, scrratch-scrritch, just like that.

MR. CARTER: And you looked inside and there was the guinea-pig – right?

MR. WILKINS: Absolutely. Beats me how it got there, though – the sides are quite high. Still, there it is. It's a weight off my mind, I can tell you.

MR. CARTER: And what have you done with it now?

MR. WILKINS: Taken it back to my room, of course – and put it in the box, where it stays till Atkinson's grandmother arrives. *And I made sure the door was shut this time, so there won't be any more of that escaping nonsense.*

MR. CARTER: I'm glad it's all ended happily. I was beginning to feel a little anxious on your behalf; in fact, I was on the point of ringing up Atkinson's grandmother and telling her not to come, till I remembered that she's probably started already.

MR. WILKINS: Don't you worry, Carter; I've got the situation under control all right. What's more, I've just been giving the brute its fodder; it's tucking into raw cabbage leaves like nobody's business.

MR. CARTER: Yes, I told Jennings and Darbishire to take it straight along to you.

MR. WILKINS: Thanks. I'd forgotten all about the feeding arrangements till Darbishire turned up with this pockets bulging with greenery.

MR. CARTER: But you couldn't have forgotten, Wilkins. Surely it was you who told them to go and find you some?

MR. WILKINS: No, I didn't: I hadn't seen them. I assumed they'd done it on your instructions.

MR. CARTER: *I* hadn't told them. This is most mysterious; they couldn't possibly have known there *was* a guinea-pig if neither of us said anything about it, so how... *(turn)* Just a minute: look out of the window, Wilkins. Do you see what I see in the headmaster's garden?

MR. WILKINS: *(turn)* Good heavens, yes! Jennings and Darbishire. *(turn back)* What on earth are they doing there?

MR. CARTER: They seem to be weeding the lettuces, judging by the way they're crawling up and down the rows.

MR. WILKINS: But – but they've no right to be there. It's out of bounds. I – I... I've got it, Carter. I shouldn't be surprised if they're not calmly helping themselves to lettuces and carrots so they can have a feast in the dormitory. Probably thought better about eating raw cabbage, so they palmed that off on me and now they've gone back for something a little more appetising.

MR. CARTER: Oh, I don't think so, Wilkins. They wouldn't do a thing like that.

MR. WILKINS: How else can you explain it? By jove, Carter, it's a good job you spotted them. *(fading)* I'm going down to the headmaster's garden to nip this green salad enterprise in the bud before it gets out of hand...

Fade out/fade in

DARBISHIRE: This is hopeless, Jennings.   I've searched these lettuces, leaf by leaf and there just isn't a whisker of F. J. Saunders anywhere.

JENNINGS: Perhaps he didn't come here after all.   I vote we go back and... Ssh!

DARBISHIRE: What did you say?

JENNINGS: I said ssh! I thought I heard something.

DARBISHIRE: Yes, so did I.

JENNINGS: What did it sound like to you?

DARBISHIRE: It was a sort of hissing noise.

JENNINGS: Don't be such a prehistoric remains, Darbi.   That was me saying ssh! Didn't you hear a sort of swooshing scritch-scratch under those rhubarb leaves? Listen!

Pause. Faint rustling of leaves

DARBISHIRE: Golly, yes, you're right.   That leaf moved just then; look, it's doing it again. *(rustle)* There's something there all right. Oh, socko, we've found F. J. Saunders at last.

JENNINGS: Quiet, Darbi! We don't want anyone to know we're here.   Now, you kneel down here in case he tries to break away on your side and I'll push the leaves back and catch him. Ready? One, two, three...

Rustling of leaves, cat miaows

Oh, goodness, it's Matron's cat!

DARBISHIRE: Oh, I say, what a swizz.   I suppose I ought to have guessed really, because Matron says she often sits among the vegetables in the afternoon.

JENNINGS: Matron does? I've never seen her.

DARBISHIRE: No, you crumbling ruin – her cat does.

JENNINGS: Oh, I see. Well, if you'd guessed really, why didn't you say so before.

DARBISHIRE: You didn't ask me before. You don't expect me to go about saying things like: "I know a vegetable patch where Matron's cat sometimes sits." You might as well expect me to go about saying: "I know a bank where the wild thyme blows."

JENNINGS: Ah, but you don't so there'd be no... oh, I say, she's hoofing off. Pick her up, Darbi.

DARBISHIRE: Come on then, Pobbles; come to uncle... Got you...

Miaow!

JENNINGS: Hang on to her, Darbi. It won't be safe to let Pobbles loose till we've found F. J. Saunders. Cats and guinea-pigs don't mix.

DARBISHIRE: Gosh, no, of course not. Yes, but supposing we don't find F. J. Saunders for hours and hours. I can't take Pobbles into class with me.

JENNINGS: We'll have to press on with the search a wizard sight quicker then. I'll look among the... oh, goodness!

DARBISHIRE: What's up – seen something?

JENNINGS: Yes.

DARBISHIRE: F. J. Saunders?

JENNINGS: No, Mr. Wilkins. He's just come through the gate; he looks as though he's going into a dive for a roof-level attack. Ssh!

MR. WILKINS: (*approaching*) Jennings and Darbishire! What on earth are you doing in the headmaster's garden? You know perfectly well it's out of bounds. Have you been picking any of these vegetables?

JENNINGS: } Oh, no, sir.

DARBISHIRE: } No, sir.

MR. WILKINS: Then why are your pockets stuffed with cabbage leaves?

JENNINGS: I didn't get those here, sir. This is the remains of the lot we got from the pig food bin that Darbishire gave you some of, sir.

MR. WILKINS: "Darbishire gave you some of!" Can't you speak English, Jennings?

JENNINGS: Yes, sir. You can have these too, if you like, only I didn't think you'd have finished eating the last lot yet, sir.

MR. WILKINS: Finished eating...! But, you silly little boy, you didn't imagine I wanted it for myself, did you?

DARBISHIRE: It did seem a little odd, sir.

MR. WILKINS: I... I... corwumph! Now look here, I've had about... What on earth are you nursing that cat for, Darbishire?

DARBISHIRE: I found her in the rhubarb, sir, and – well, I didn't think it was safe to let her wander about just at present.

MR. WILKINS: Not safe! But the cat's perfectly harmless. Anyone would think it was a man-eating tiger. I've had enough of this trumpery moonshine and breaking bounds with armfuls of cat. (*going*) Go up to my room and wait for me there. I'm going to get to the bottom of this business or know the reason why.

JENNINGS: Yes, sir – come along, Darbishire...

Fade out/fade in on miaows

DARBISHIRE: How much longer have I got to go on carrying this cat, Jennings? She's getting heavier and heavier every step I take.

JENNINGS: Pull yourself together, Darbi. She can't really be getting heavier.

DARBISHIRE: Well, I must be getting lighter, then. Here's Wilkie's room, thank goodness. I'll put her down now. F. J. Saunders isn't likely to be around these parts. Down you go, Pobbles. (*departing miaow*)

JENNINGS: Wilkie did tell us to wait *in*side his room, didn't he?

DARBISHIRE: Yes, I think so.

JENNINGS: (*going*) Come along then. Of course, we'll have to tell him everything now, worse luck, and there'll be the most frantic... (*door opens*) Golly, Darbishire! Here he is... I've found him!

DARBISHIRE: Who?

JENNINGS: Good old F. J. Saunders, as large as life and hopping about by the fireplace.

DARBISHIRE: I say, how socko! But however did he get in here?

JENNINGS: I don't know. Perhaps he smelled Wilkie's raw cabbage and beetled in for a quick snack when no one was looking.

DARBISHIRE: Goodness! Wouldn't Mr. Wilkins be in a bate if he knew there was a guinea-pig in his room! We'd better get Saunders out of here quickly before he comes up and finds him.

JENNINGS: Yes, but we'll have to find somewhere a wizard sight safer this time: he's too clever at escaping. Now if only we'd got a cage or something.

DARBISHIRE: I know where there is one: it's a parrot cage actually, but it'd do for now, wouldn't it?

JENNINGS: Yes, rather! Where is it?

JENNINGS: It's Mr. Wilkins. He looks as though he's going into a dive for a roof-level attack.

DARBISHIRE: Upstairs in the attic. I saw it last week. I had special permish from Mr. Carter to go there. Come on, Jen; you take F. J. Saunders in your pocket and I'll... (*miaow!*) Oh, heavens, Pobbles has wandered in!

JENNINGS: Well, leave her here. She won't do any harm. We haven't got time for her now, because we'll have to be jolly quick. If we can get it all fixed before Wilkie comes up, we may be able to keep F. J. Saunders on the secret list after all. Righto, I've got him – lead the way upstairs.

Fade out/fade in

DARBISHIRE: I can't get over running him to earth in Mr. Wilkie's room. It's not a spot I'd choose to roost in even with cabbage laid on. Now, if he'd made for the tuck-shop, for instance...

JENNINGS: Don't natter, Darbi. We've got no time to lose, and if we're not back in Wilkie's room by the time he gets there, we shall be lost.

DARBISHIRE: Lost? Don't be crazy; I know my way round the attics blindfold.

JENNINGS: I mean the game will be up if he finds us there.

DARBISHIRE: Oh, I see. You mean if we're found, we're lost. That doesn't make sense, does it. My father says that...

JENNINGS: Here we are. Heavens, what a lot of junk they keep in school attics.

DARBISHIRE: There's the parrot cage, look, right up on the top of that old cupboard. It'll be just the job, won't it?

JENNINGS: Yes, I'll climb up and get it. I'll have to move this old bedstead first.

Ad lib and bumps and thuds

DARBISHIRE: Ssh! Don't make such a row. We're out of bounds, don't forget, and if anyone hears us...

JENNINGS: Shut the door then.

DARBISHIRE: (*going*) Righto.

Door squeaks shut

JENNINGS: Now let's get on with it. You hold this old bed steady.

DARBISHIRE: Hold the what?

JENNINGS: I said: "Hold this old bed steady".

DARBISHIRE: You mean bedstead, don't you? There's no such thing as a bed*steady*.

JENNINGS: I mean, hold the bedstead steady while I climb up and get the parrot-cage...

DARBISHIRE: Oh, I see.

JENNINGS: That's the idea... I can't quite reach. I shall have to... Oh, I say, Darbi – look, through the window. Mr. Wilkins is coming across the quad with Mr. Carter.

DARBISHIRE: Oh, fish-hooks, that means he's going up to his room to see if we're there. We'll have to hare downstairs like blinko if we're going to get there first.

JENNINGS: I can't come yet – I've still got F. J. Saunders in my pocket. You nip on ahead, Darbi, and tell Wilkie I'm coming.

DARBISHIRE: Righto. (*going*) I'll try and keep the conversation going smoothly about this and that till you're...

Door handle rattled, faint thud off

(*coming back*) Oh, goodness, oh, fish-hooks!

JENNINGS: Now what's up?

DARBISHIRE: The door knob – it's come away in my hand.

JENNINGS: Well, put it back again and get weaving.

DARBISHIRE: I can't. The screw came out when I pulled it off, and I heard the other end fall down doyoyng in the passage outside. It was the business end too, with the spindle thing on.

JENNINGS: Here, let me have a look.

Door rattled

DARBISHIRE: It's no good shaking it, Jen. You can only open it from the outside. Oh, why do these things always pick on us? You'd think that with a whole school full of chaps it'd be someone else's turn to get a...

JENNINGS: We'll have to attract someone's attention or we never *shall* get out. I've got it! How about letting something down out of the window on a piece of string and swinging it so it goes boink on the window just below?

DARBISHIRE: Oh, good wheeze! What shall we use?

JENNINGS: We want something we can tap heavily on the glass with. There's the parrot cage, of course. It's not what you'd call the ideal window-tapper, but it'll do.

DARBISHIRE: Okay, then; get it down. And for goodness sake be quick.

JENNINGS: The trouble is, I can't remember whose window is just below this one.

DARBISHIRE: I can; it's Matron's room – I'm pretty sure of that.

JENNINGS: Oh, good; she won't mind.

DARBISHIRE: At least, I *think* it's Matron's room; or rather, it might be Matron's room. Well, anyway, let's hope it is...

Fade out/fade in

MR. WILKINS: ...and quite frankly, Carter, I couldn't make head or tail of what Jennings and Darbishire *were* doing in the headmaster's garden, but I'll soon find out. They're waiting outside my room for me now.

MR. CARTER: They're not, Wilkins. The corridor's empty.

MR. WILKINS: Eh? Well, that's odd. I sent them ahead while I...

MR. CARTER: And what's more, Wilkins, your door is wide open.

MR. WILKINS: What!! Good heavens, so it is. What about that wretched guinea-pig; he'll escape. Come on, Carter, quickly, we've got to stop it getting out at all costs... *(turn)* Now, I left it in this - ... No, oh no! It's got out – it's gone – the box is empty!

MR. CARTER: And your armchair is full.

MR. WILKINS: Eh?

MR. CARTER: Full of cat. Purring happily and looking very pleased with itself. H'm, I'm afraid it means Atkinson's grandmother has seen the last of her pet.

MR. WILKINS: Yes, but dash it all, Carter, I mean...

MR. CARTER: On the other hand, we haven't seen the last of Atkinson's grandmother. Here's the village taxi coming across the quad, and it's pretty obvious who's inside. You'll have to go and explain to her, Wilkins, that owing to an unfortunate accident the guinea-pig got out and...

MR. WILKINS: Yes, but how did the cat get *in*? The door was closed. I distinctly remember... Wait – I see what's happened; it's that wretched Jennings and Darbishire! They'd got the cat with them. They must have opened the door and walked off. I think they're going off their heads. Would you believe it, they actually thought I wanted that cabbage for myself: can you imagine anything more fantastic!

Tapping on window, continue at intervals to end of fade

Good heavens, what on earth's that?

MR. CARTER: It's something outside your window, Wilkins. It looks like – yes, it is! It's a parrot cage let down from above on a piece of string.

MR. WILKINS: Parrot cage! I... I... corwumph! If that's Jennings and Darbishire up to their tricks again, I'll... I'll... well, they'd better look out.

MR. CARTER: It's certainly rather extraordinary. I should go up to the attic and find out what it's all about if I were you, Wilkins. It does answer your question, though.

MR. WILKINS: What question, Carter?

MR. CARTER: You asked me whether I could imagine anything more fantastic than the idea of your tucking into raw cabbage. I should say that beating a tattoo on your window with a suspended parrot cage must run it pretty close.

MR. WILKINS: Cor-wumph! I'll soon put a stop to this. I'll...

MR. CARTER: In the meantime, I'll slip down and ask Atkinson's grandmother to wait. But I think I'll leave it to you to break the sad news.

MR. WILKINS: Oh, I say, dash it Carter, you wouldn't do a thing like that!

MR. CARTER: I'm sorry, Wilkins, but the guinea-pig was your pigeon, wasn't it?

MR. WILKINS: I... I... corwumph. When I get hold of Jennings and Darbishire, I...

Fade to

(*approaching*) Who's in this room? Open this door at once!

JENNINGS: (*off*) We can't, sir. We're marooned. The knob's fallen out on your side.

MR. WILKINS: Eh? Oh, so it has. I'll soon have this door open and then perhaps you'll be good enough to explain... There!

Replacing of knob, door opens

JENNINGS: (*normal*) Oh, thank you, sir. It's awfully decent of you to rescue us.

MR. WILKINS: Now look here, Jennings: what on earth were you doing in this attic?

JENNINGS: Trying to get out, sir.

MR. WILKINS: Yes, I know that, you silly little boy. But what did you want to go in for?

JENNINGS: Well, it's like this, sir. You said we'd got to report to you... and so we...

MR. WILKINS: You didn't expect to find me in the attic, did you?

JENNINGS: No, sir. But you see we'd got Pobbles with us and we didn't think it was safe so we came up here to get the parrot cage.

MR. WILKINS: What did you want to put the cat in the parrot cage for?

JENNINGS: Oh, we didn't, sir. Perhaps I'd better explain. You see, you know there's a rule about pets, sir, well...

MR. CARTER: (*approaching*) Ah, there you are, Wilkins. Atkinson's grandmother's waiting for you in the drawing-room. She seems a bit – ah – well I should advise you to break the sad news as tactfully as you can.

MR. WILKINS: You know it really is too bad, Carter. If these silly little boys hadn't left my door open... it's all their fault.

MR. CARTER: I'm afraid it is. You two boys have caused more trouble than you realise by not doing as you were told. Furthermore, it's the second time since lunch. I distinctly told you, Jennings, to empty your pockets, and now look at them! They're bulging as much as ever and I... good heavens, Jennings, whatever *have* you got in your pocket? It's moving!

JENNINGS: Yes, I know, sir. I was going to explain – it's only a – well, it's this, sir.

MR. WILKINS: The guinea-pig! Well, I... I... What on earth is it doing in your pocket?

JENNINGS: I just put it there till the cage was ready, sir. It wouldn't have been safe to use it as a window-tapper with F. J. Saunders inside.

MR. CARTER: Who, Jennings?

JENNINGS: That's my guinea-pig's name, sir.

MR. WILKINS: *Your* guinea-pig! Don't be ridiculous, boy – it's *my* guinea-pig.

JENNINGS: But, sir, it can't be – I found it.

MR. WILKINS: And I lost it!

JENNINGS: *You* did, sir?

DARBISHIRE: Oh, golly: that explains lots of things. If only we'd known you were a guinea-pig fancier, sir – well, fancy that. Or rather, I don't mean fancy the guinea-pig, I mean...

MR. CARTER: We'll leave the explanations till afterwards, Darbishire. Meanwhile, I suggest we put the guinea-pig in

111

the parrot cage and make Atkinson's grandmother a present of the whole lot.

MR. WILKINS: Good idea, Carter. Pop him in the cage, Jennings.

JENNINGS: Oh, but aren't you going to keep him for yourself, sir?

DARBISHIRE: Yes, I thought you fancied guinea-pigs, sir.

MR. WILKINS: No, Darbishire, I only fancied I'd lost one, and the sooner I *do* lose it to its rightful owner the better.

MR. CARTER: She's waiting for you in the drawing-room, Wilkins.

MR. WILKINS: Yes, yes, yes, coming now. (*Going with Carter ad lib*) But I tell you, Carter, if I had my way I'd go a bit further than prohibiting pets on the premises during term time: I wouldn't allow grandmothers on the premises either.

DARBISHIRE: (*shocked to the core*) Jennings! Did you hear what he said?

JENNINGS: (*slowly*) Just like Old Wilkie. Fancy saying mouldy things like that about decent things like pets and grandmothers. Now, if he'd said he wouldn't allow any masters on the premises in term time, then things *would* begin to look up!

Fade out. Music.

Linbury Court Preparatory School

Dear David,

   As it is getting near the end of term
Darbishire and I decided to write a famous end of
term play. It was a very good play about a miser
with a moustache but the moustache got sent to
the cleaner's by mistake with Darbishire's best
suit, so we had to scrap it and do Henry V
instead, although our play was a lot better
really, especially as Mr Wilkins refused to wear
a brass coal scuttle for a helmet and we had to
get an understudy. But it was all right on the
night.

   Must stop now owing to shortage of blotch, but
will reveal all on Wed.
Yours very sincely,

J.C.T. Jennings.

JENNINGS
TAKES THE STAGE

(Fourth series no.7 – request week)

(No.6 of the fourth series was a new production of
Jennings Takes the Cake)

Jennings Takes the Stage was the twenty-sixth Jennings play.

It was first broadcast by the BBC Home Service for Children's Hour
on 5th April 1952 with the following cast:

JENNINGS	John Charlesworth
DARBISHIRE	Henry Searle
MR. CARTER	Geoffrey Wincott
MR. WILKINS	Wilfred Babbage
VENABLES	Jeremy Spenser
TEMPLE	Malcolm Hillier
ATKINSON	Wilfrid Downing
MATRON	Peggy Cameron
IRVING BORROWMORE	Ralph de Rohan

Produced by David Davis

(*The version that follows is taken from the script broadcast on 12/12/57*)

Music. Fade in, door opens

MR. CARTER: Ah, there you are, Wilkins. I thought I might run you to earth in the staff room.

MR. WILKINS: Oh, hullo, Carter. Don't interrupt, there's a good chap. I'm up to my eyes in end-of-term reports. (*quoting to himself*) "Atkinson – very fair – has made progress. Darbishire – very fair – has made progress. Jennings – very..." No, no. I'd better put something quite different this time. What about: "Has made progress; very fair"?

MR. CARTER: That'd certainly make a change. Anyway, Wilkins, I looked in to see what you're doing about the little informal concert for the last night of term. There's only tomorrow left, you know, and you did say you'd organise it, if you remember?

MR. WILKINS: Yes, yes, yes, I know; and you needn't worry, Carter. I've got everything arranged. I've written and asked Mr. Irving Borrowmore to come down and entertain us with some of his dramatic recitations.

MR. CARTER: You've asked whom?

MR. WILKINS: Irving Borrowmore, the actor. He does character studies from Dickens and Shakespeare and that sort of thing. He's very good, too. You know – "Is this a dagger which I see before me? Is this a..."

MR. CARTER: No Wilkins, it's a fountain pen to remind you that you've a lot more reports to finish yet. All the same, you know, I don't think the headmaster will approve of engaging a professional actor just for our little end-of-term party. He's keen on the boys putting on something themselves.

MR. WILKINS: Oh. Oh, I see. Well, if that's what he thinks I'd better ring up and cancel Irving Borrowmore, and let the boys get on with it. But I tell you, Carter, I've got no time to run around organising things; I must get on with my reports... "Temple – has made very fair progress... Venables..."

Door knock

MR. CARTER: Come in.

Door opens/shuts

JENNINGS: (*approaching*) Oh, please, sir...

MR. CARTER: Well, Jennings, what can I do for you?

JENNINGS: Well, sir, it's about the concert, sir. Darbishire and I want to do a play we wrote while we were making our beds this morning. You see, Darbishire's got a false moustache, so we thought that if you'd lend us the starting pistol you use for the sports, sir, we could do a play about an old miser with a moustache who gets shot, sir.

MR. CARTER: Oh dear, must we have an untidy litter of corpses all over the stage?

JENNINGS: Yes, sir, we've got to shoot the miser so's someone else can wear the moustache in Scene 2, sir. We're going to stick it on with stamp hinges so that it will come off quickly. And after this second chap wears it and gets shot and goes off, sir, a policeman comes on in Scene 3. And this time *he's* got the moustache, so he has a fight with the villain and then he gets away, so that...

MR. CARTER: So that a further moustachioed character can come along and get shot in Scene 4! Right?

JENNINGS: Yes, sir. You see, the villain knows the police are after him, so in Scene 5 he grows a moustache to disguise himself; so, when the police see him in Scene 6, they just think: "Here comes a man with a moustache," but in Scene 7 he shaves it off again, so the detective can wear it in Scene 8, when they start shooting each other within an inch of their lives, sir. It's super exciting, sir, because the first bullet whistles through the bristles...

MR. CARTER: Who's wearing the false moustache now?

JENNINGS: The detective, sir; but in Scene 9, the moustache is going to be handed...

MR. WILKINS: Doh! I – I – Corwumph! I wish you'd stop talking about false moustaches when I'm trying to concentrate on reports. Look what you've made me put! "Has made very fair moustache." I – I...

JENNINGS: Sorry, sir. It's not a very fair moustache, really, though.

MR. WILKINS: What!

JENNINGS: No, sir. It's a black, droopy one like Chinamen have, so in scene 10 they all go to China...

MR. WILKINS: No look here, Jennings, I don't mind where they go, so long as they don't come in here cluttering the place knee-deep with droopy-moustached Chinamen while I'm trying to write reports.

MR. CARTER: We mustn't disturb Mr. Wilkins, Jennings.

JENNINGS: No, sir.

117

MR. CARTER: In any case, I don't like your play at all. Couldn't you choose something fairly straightforward – a short scene from Shakespeare, for instance?

JENNINGS: (*unwillingly*) I suppose we *could*, sir. Er – did Hamlet have a moustache, sir?

MR. CARTER: No, Jennings.

JENNINGS: Oh – well, that washes Hamlet out – thank goodness! I suppose we couldn't do the murder of Julius Caesar with the starting pistol, could we, sir? Brutus or someone could wear the moustache.

MR. CARTER: No, Jennings. And I suggest you stop trying to fit Shakespeare into your false moustache. Never mind the properties – the play's the thing.

JENNINGS: Yes, sir. Well, I'll think it over, sir, but I know Darbishire and the others won't like it. They're rehearsing in the class-room, and they won't want to scrap a supersonic play like ours just for Shakespeare, sir.

Fade out/fade in

DARBISHIRE: Now if you chaps are ready, we'll start rehearsing Scene 1. You're the villain, Temple, and you're the old miser with the moustache, Venables. Only you'll have to pretend for now, because it's upstairs in my other jacket.

TEMPLE: What about my gun, Darbishire?

DARBISHIRE: Jennings has gone to ask Mr. Carter if we can borrow the starting pistol. Here's an old busted pop-gun you can practise with, to be going on with. And this is a cardboard dagger I've made, just to make things look more exciting.

TEMPLE: Coo, thanks, Darbishire.

DARBISHIRE: Now, let's get cracking. You come on first, Temple, and here's what you say in this notebook.

TEMPLE: Righto. (*Exaggerated 'stage' voice*) *"Creeping on stealthily, I wonder if I shall meet that old miser, Mr. Brown, today."*

DARBISHIRE: No, you bazooka! You don't *say* "Creeping on stealthily". That's what you have to *do*.

TEMPLE: Oh, sorry. *"I wonder if I shall meet that old miser, Mr. Brown, today. Yes, there he is; now is my chance."*

DARBISHIRE: Now you come on, Venables, smelling of moth balls and looking as though you've just hidden your secret hoard under the floorboards of your house at 231 High Street.

VENABLES: Wow! That sounds a bit tricky.

DARBISHIRE: Oh shut up, Venables. Go on, Temple. "Now is my chance."

TEMPLE: *"Now is my chance. I will speak to him."* (*Calling loudly.*) *"Hem-hem! ... Hem-hem!..."*

VENABLES: If you're talking to me, Temple, you've got the name wrong. *I'm* not Hem-hem. Darbi said my name was Mr. Brown, the old miser.

TEMPLE: I'm only reading what it says here. Perhaps Hem-hem is your nickname, or something. Mr. Hem-hem Brown.

DARBISHIRE: No, no, no, you bazookas! Hem-hem isn't his name – it's just a throat-clearing noise. You want to attract his attention, Temple, so you cough – hem, hem.

TEMPLE: But I haven't got a cough.

DARBISHIRE: Well pretend you have!

Paroxysm of coughing. Door opens

Oh, there you are, Jennings. Have you got the starting pistol?

JENNINGS: No. Mr. Carter won't lend it.

TEMPLE: Oh heavens! What are we going to do then? I can't shoot anyone with this busted pop-gun. It won't make a noise.

JENNINGS: All right, all right – don't get in a flap. I've brought these paper bags along, so when you want to shoot, just point the gun at him. I'll stand in the wings and blow a bag up and burst it. Like this – look!

Blowing into bag, successful explosion, reaction

TEMPLE: Oh, golly wizzo. Sounds just like a revolver.

JENNINGS: Yes, but it doesn't always work, so you'd better be ready to jump on Venables and stab him, just in case.

Reaction

DARBISHIRE: Come on, then; let's get on with it.

TEMPLE: Righto. (*stage voice*) *"Hem-hem! Good morning, Mr. Brown. Nice day is it not?"*

VENABLES: (*stage voice*) *"Ah-ha! I recognise you. I presume you are my worst enemy, Mr. Percy Robinson, who wishes to steal the secret hoard of bank notes which I've just hidden under the floorboards in my bedroom, three feet from the window, in the house where I live, Number 231 High Street, are you not?"*

TEMPLE: What do you mean, "Are you not?" Am I not *what*?

VENABLES: I don't know. You'd better ask Jennings. He wrote this play. I'm just reading what it says here; I suppose it means are you not my worst enemy who wishes to steal the secret hoard...

TEMPLE: All right, we've done that bit. Let's get on with the shooting. It may liven up a bit then. There's too much hem-heming and ah-ha-ing in this play for my liking. (*In stage voice.*) "*So we meet again, Mr. Brown! You are about to breathe your last.*"

VENABLES: Breathe my last *what*?

DARBISHIRE: Never mind *what* – just breathe it! We'll never get through the first scene if you keep stopping to ask silly questions. Go on, Temple.

TEMPLE: (*stage voice*) "*Breathe your last and breathe it quickly, for I have here a .22 automatic sharpshooter with which I propose to shoot you.*"

VENABLES: (*stage voice*) "*Help, help; do not shoot, Mr. Robinson... Have mercy, Percy!*"

TEMPLE: "*Too late; my finger is on the trigger...*"

Blowing up of paper bag

"*My finger is on the trigger... My finger is on the trigger...*"

Bag blowing

(*normal voice*) Well, for heaven's sake, Jennings, hurry up and burst that bag. I can't keep my finger on the trigger all night.

JENNINGS: (*puffing*) You'll have to wait; these bags take a lot of breath. This job's worse than breathing your last.

Blowing into bag

TEMPLE: "*My finger is on the trigger.*"

Blowing into bag

DARBISHIRE: (*calling*) All right, all right. Never mind the gun, Temple. Use your dagger.

TEMPLE: Okay. Here we go, then. "*Now, Mr. Brown, I hereby stab you in the back.*"

Loud report as bag bursts at last

VENABLES: "*Ah-ha! False villain. You have stabbed me – I mean, you have shot me.*" Oh, I say, this is feeble. I don't know whether I've been stabbed or shot now.

JENNINGS: (*coming up*) Sorry, I was a bit late with the bang, but it looked super exciting, didn't it, Darbi?

VENABLES: *"Ah-ha! False villain. You have stabbed me – I mean, you have shot me."*

DARBISHIRE: Smashing! Now let's do Scene... Oh, we can't do Scene 2 till Atkinson turns up. I vote we go up to the dorm and get the moustache while we're waiting.

JENNINGS: I'll come with you, Darbi. You others stay here. We shan't be long.

Fade out/fade in

DARBISHIRE: Here we are. I'll get my best suit out of my locker and then we ought to be all right. (*going*) Hold on a minute.

Locker opened, off

(*approaching, off*) That's funny; it's gone!

JENNINGS: It can't have.

DARBISHIRE: Look for yourself. I left it folded up on this shelf with the moustache in the pocket.

JENNINGS: Perhaps Matron knows where it is. There she is, look, getting the trunks ready for packing. Let's go and ask her.

DARBISHIRE: Matron!

MATRON: (*approaching*) Hullo, Darbishire. What can I do for you?

DARBISHIRE: Matron, my best suit's gone out of my locker.

MATRON: Quite right. I've sent it to the cleaners.

JENNINGS: The cleaners! Oh, fish-hooks!

MATRON: You'll have to travel home in your other one.

DARBISHIRE: Oh, but, Matron, that's no good. I must have my best suit now; there's something urgent in the pocket.

JENNINGS: Heavens! This has bished things up nicely. The whole play will be ruined if we don't get it back. I wonder if - I say, Matron, would you do me a favour, please?

MATRON: It depends on what it is, Jennings.

JENNINGS: Would you ring up the manager of the cleaners and ask him whether he's got a moustache?

MATRON: That sounds a rather personal question to ask anyone on the phone. As a matter of fact, I seem to remember he's clean-shaven.

JENNINGS: Oh, I don't mean him personally, Matron. It's Darbishire's moustache I'm worried about.

MATRON: Darbishire's! Oh, I don't think you need bother about that for some years yet, do you, Darbishire?

DARBISHIRE: No, you don't understand, Matron. It's a *false* one for the concert we're talking about. Of course, I know it's about time it was sent to the cleaners, really, but what are we going to do without it?

JENNINGS: Mouldy chizz! We'll have to scrap the whole play, that's all. We can't possibly do a play about a man who comes on in a moustache and gets shot if we haven't got a moustache for him to come on in.

DARBISHIRE: Oh dear, what a ghastly catastrophe. Why do these things always happen to us? My father says that Shakespeare says that when sorrows come they come not...

JENNINGS: Never mind about Shakespeare. I had enough trouble with him when Mr. Carter tried to persuade me to do one of his plays instead of ours.

DARBISHIRE: I didn't know Mr. Carter had written any plays.

JENNINGS: Shakespeare's plays, you clodpoll! Mr. Carter thinks Shakespeare's plays are better than ours.

DARBISHIRE: I don't see how it *can* be better. Why, they don't even have .22 guns in Shakespeare.

MATRON: All the same, Mr. Carter may be right, you know. Why not give Shakespeare a chance? Weren't you studying a scene in class last week?

JENNINGS: Yes, we were, Matron; it was a chunk of Henry V. But we couldn't do that – we haven't got any costumes.

MATRON: If there aren't too many of you in it, I might be able to run up something for you to wear from these odd pieces in the sewing-room.

JENNINGS: Oh, wacko, Matron! Would you really? That'd be smashing, wouldn't it, Darbi?

DARBISHIRE: Yes, rather. Real costumes – super wacko! Just for the five of us – that's all we need, Matron.

MATRON: All right, then. Come and see me about it tomorrow.

JENNINGS: Oh thanks, Matron! We'll have to do that bit just before the battle of Agincourt, where the King comes on and makes that supersonic speech. And we could still use the paper bags for the cannon balls going off in the background.

DARBISHIRE: Yes, and we ought to have a fanfare for when the King comes on.

JENNINGS: What! – Roundabouts and coconut-shies and things? Surely you wouldn't expect to find a funfair at the battle of Agincourt?

DARBISHIRE: I didn't say a *funfair*: I said a fanfare, you prehistoric ruin.

JENNINGS: Oh, I see.

DARBISHIRE: I've got a tin trumpet in my tuck box that'd do wizardly.

JENNINGS: Righto, go and get it. I'll get the Shakespeare books from the classroom and then we'll get on with the rehearsal.

Fade/fade in

TEMPLE: Come on, Jennings and Darbishire. You've been ages.

JENNINGS: Sorry, chaps. We've had to alter our plans because we've lost the moustache. We're going to do a hunk of Henry V instead. Act 4, Scene 3 – just before the battle of Agincourt. Matron and Mr. Carter seem to think it's better than ours.

DARBISHIRE: And we're only doing the one scene, so that'll make things a lot easier.

Reaction

JENNINGS: Now, let's see: there's Bedford and Exeter, Salisbury and Gloucester, Warwick and...

ATKINSON: I thought you said there was only one scene. That's five places already.

JENNINGS: Those aren't *places*, Atkinson, you coot; those are *people*. They just call themselves after places.

VENABLES: That's crazy. Why call yourself Bedford and Exeter? Why not Burton-on-Trent or Weston-Super-Mare?

DARBISHIRE: Because they're *barons*, don't you see! They're allowed to call themselves after counties.

TEMPLE: Well, you're not a baron, so why do you call yourself Darbishire?

DARBISHIRE: Ah, that's different. My father says that our family was originally descended from the...

JENNINGS: All right, Darbi, all right. Now, let's see how we're going to dish these parts out. You can be the Duke of Gloucester, Venables; you're the Duke of Exeter, Temple...

TEMPLE: Has it got to be Exeter? Couldn't it be Bournemouth, instead, because I went there last holidays...

JENNINGS: No, it couldn't. There isn't a Duke of Bournemouth in the play. Now, Darbi and Atkinson and I can be the other three barons, and there we are.

ATKINSON: That's all very well, but you've forgotten Henry V. We can't do without him, unless we alter the play quite a lot.

DARBISHIRE: Yes, and it's a terribly long part. We'll need someone with a supersonic memory to learn all those speeches.

125

JENNINGS: Yes, I hadn't thought of that. And he's only got till this time tomorrow to learn it in.

TEMPLE: Well, somebody's got to do it. Who's got a supersonic memory?

JENNINGS: Mr. Wilkins!

Incredulous reaction

ATKINSON: Fish-hooks, no! Not Old Wilkie! I wouldn't cast him for the back legs of a pantomime horse, let alone a character like Henry V.

JENNINGS: I think Old Wilkie would be jolly good. He's always telling us how easy it is to learn things off by heart, and here's his chance.

DARBISHIRE: Yes, that's not a bad idea.

TEMPLE: He ought to be jolly proud at being asked. And we'll keep it top priority secret, shall we? Then all the audience will think some ordinary form three-er, like Binns minor, is going to come on and – oh goodness, won't they get a surprise!

VENABLES: We'd better ask Mr. Wilkins first, though.

JENNINGS: All right, I will. Now, let's get on with the scene up to where the King comes in. Got your trumpet, Darbi?

DARBISHIRE: Yes, here it is.

Tin trumpet blasts, reaction: What a ghastly row, etc.

TEMPLE: That sounds terrible, Darbi.

DARBISHIRE: Well, you come and do better, then. It sounded jolly good to me, and I ought to know, because my father says I've got a very musical ear, and I'll probably become a famous musician one day, and perhaps I'll even be asked to play at the Royal Festival...

JENNINGS: All right, all right, get on with it. Don't just stand there blowing your trumpet.

DARBISHIRE: That's just what you told me to stand here and *do*. How can I sound my famous fanfare if I can't blow my own trumpet?

JENNINGS: Well, *blow* your own trumpet, then, but for goodness sake don't do it so loud. The last one went in one ear and it hasn't come out of the other yet.

DARBISHIRE: All right. Stand by.

Trumpet blasts, door opens

MR. WILKINS: (*approaching*) What on earth's going on in here!

Who was making that horrible ear-splitting noise?

DARBISHIRE: I was, sir. It was my famous fanfare.

MR. WILKINS: Oh, was it. It sounded more like a shower of stones on a tin roof. If you boys can't amuse yourselves without making all that noise, you won't be allowed to come in here.

JENNINGS: Oh, sir, Mr. Wilkins, sir. You're just the person we wanted, sir. Will you very kindly do us a favour, sir?

MR. WILKINS: It depends what it is.

JENNINGS: Well you see, sir, we've had to scrap our play because of Darbishire's moustache going off to the cleaners. So we're going to do Shakespeare, instead.

MR. WILKINS: I don't see what it's got to do with me.

JENNINGS: Well, sir, we wondered whether you'd very kindly play Henry V for us in the concert tomorrow night. You see, it's too long for us to learn; and I'm sure you'd be jolly good and the audience would get a surprise, wouldn't they, sir?

MR. WILKINS: Why should they be surprised if I'm good?

JENNINGS: Oh, I didn't mean that, sir.

MR. WILKINS: I should hope not indeed.

DARBISHIRE: Still, if it's too difficult for you, sir...

MR. WILKINS: Too difficult! Don't be ridiculous, boy. Why, I could play a part like that on my head, if I wanted to.

JENNINGS: We wouldn't want to surprise the audience all that much, sir; if you'd just play it the right way up, that'd be good enough for us. Here's where it starts, sir. Top of the page.

MR. WILKINS: H'm. Yes, I see. All right: how's this?

(*woodenly*) *"What's he that wishes so?*

My cousin Westmoreland? – no my fair cousin;

If we are markt to die, we are enow to do our country loss,

And if to live, the fewer men the greater share of honour. "

JENNINGS: } Oh, jolly good, sir!

DARBISHIRE: } Smashing, wasn't it!

TEMPLE: } Wow, sir! I never knew you were such a jolly wizard actor, sir!

ATKINSON: } You ought to be on the radio, sir!

MR. WILKINS: H'm, yes, I suppose it wasn't too bad for a first effort. All right, I'll play King Henry for you. But you'll have to rehearse without me; I shan't have time for that. I'll have a look at the part later on this evening. I don't suppose it'll take me more than a few minutes to learn.

ATKINSON: Wow! Won't it really, sir? Not many people could learn all that in a few minutes. You must have got a twelve horse-power brain, sir.

MR. WILKINS: It's quite easy, if you put your mind to it.

JENNINGS: Yes, all right, sir. Thanks very much. Jolly lobsterous of you, sir. And you won't tell anyone, will you? We want it to be a surprise, sir.

MR. WILKINS: You leave that to me. I can't stay now; I've got some more reports to finish. (*going*) And for goodness sake don't play any more of those horrible fun fairs – fanfares!

Door shuts

JENNINGS: Well, that's settled, thank goodness. Now we'd better be getting on with our bits.

DARBISHIRE: Yes, we mustn't waste any time. This time tomorrow we'll be getting ready to go on the stage.

Fade out/fade in

MATRON: Here you are, Darbishire; this is your costume. Put it on carefully.

DARBISHIRE: Ooh, thank you, Matron. It's super.

MATRON: And here's yours, Jennings. You other boys will find yours on your beds.

JENNINGS: Thank you, Matron.

MATRON: No, Jennings, you're putting it on upside down... There, that's better.

DARBISHIRE: Just look at my armour-plating! Do I look like the Earl of Westmoreland, Matron?

MATRON: I couldn't have told you apart, Darbishire.

VENABLES: Goodo! I'm jolly excited. Five minutes to go and then it starts.

TEMPLE: Yes, the audience are going in to the hall already. Goodness, won't they get a surprise when Henry V comes on! Of course, you know who it is, don't you, Matron?

MATRON: I've no idea, Temple

TEMPLE: But you *must* know, Matron, because – well, what about his costume?

MATRON: I hope he's quite small, whoever it is. There's only this little coat-of-mail left.

ATKINSON: Oh, *Matron*! Mr. Wilkins will never be able to get into a titchy little tunic like that!

128

MATRON: Mr. Wilkins! Surely he's not playing King Henry!

TEMPLE: Yes, Matron. Didn't Jennings tell you?

MATRON: No: this is the first I've heard of it. Oh dear, I don't know what you can do. I've nothing at all that would fit a grown-up the size of Mr. Wilkins. Why didn't you tell me before, Jennings?

JENNINGS: I'm terribly sorry, Matron. But you see, it was a secret, so I thought you'd be sure to know.

TEMPLE: You are a prize bazooka, Jennings. You've ruined the whole show. You can't have Henry V coming on in a hairy tweed jacket and flannel trousers. What'll people think?

JENNINGS: We'll just have to think of something for him, that's all.

VENABLES: (*in panic*) But there's no time. The audience are going in!

JENNINGS: Oh, heavens! Well, I wonder if he'd mind wearing this red blanket off my bed. He could sort of drape it round his shoulders.

ATKINSON: Don't be crazy. He'd look like a Red Indian Chief!

JENNINGS: Well, it's better than nothing. And for a helmet he could wear – well, he could wear...

TEMPLE: Well, what? There just isn't anything.

JENNINGS: Yes, there is. There's a brass coal scuttle in the sick room.

DARBISHIRE: But it's not even clean. It'd make him all coally. Honestly, Jen, you've cooked up the worst bish in history. Here's the whole school ready and waiting for a super Shakespeare production, and Henry V comes on in a red blanket and a coat scuttle.

VENABLES: You are a clodpoll, Jennings. You've spoilt everything. And after Mr. Wilkins has learnt his part specially on purpose, too.

JENNINGS: Well, it's too late to do anything about it now. You chaps go down and get on the stage, and I'll take Mr. Wilkins his coal scuttle. Oh goodness, I do hope it fits him.

                 Fade out, fade in, door opens

MR. CARTER: (*approaching*) Ah, there you are, Wilkins. Coming along to see the concert?

MR. WILKINS: I wish I could, Carter, but as a matter of fact I'm in a spot of trouble. I just don't know what to do.

MR. CARTER: Oh?

MR. WILKINS: Yes, I rashly agreed to play Henry V when the boys asked me yesterday afternoon.

MR. CARTER: Splendid, Wilkins! This explains the mysterious rumours that have been sweeping through the school all day. It was obvious that something very special was being planned for tonight. Well, well! Mind you're good, Wilkins. The boys are expecting an outstanding performance.

MR. WILKINS: Yes, yes, yes, but what I'm trying to tell you is that I don't know the part.

MR. CARTER: You don't know it?

MR. WILKINS: Not more than the first few lines, anyway. I've been so busy with these wretched reports that I haven't had time to learn it.

MR. CARTER: Well, it's a bit late in the day to say that. You're due on the stage in a few minutes.

MR. WILKINS: (*in complete panic*) I can't go on! I can't go on, Carter; it's impossible. There's about fifty lines in this speech and all I know is the first three. Let's see, how do they go. Er?

"What's he that wishes so?
My cousin Westmoreland? No, my fair cousin,
If we are – er – if we are something-or-other,
We are enow to – er – to – er... "

Oh, it's hopeless, Carter. I just don't know it at all. I wish I could think of a way to get out of it.

MR. CARTER: I don't see how you possibly can now, with the audience sitting there waiting. It's a pity I asked you to ring up and put off Mr. Irving Borrowmore's visit.

MR. WILKINS: *What!* Oh, good heavens! I've just remembered. That's another thing I haven't done. I completely forgot all about cancelling it. Oh, this is awful, Carter! He may be turning up at any moment. It's bad enough making an undignified exhibition of yourself in front of a lot of little boys; but if we're going to have professional Shakespearian actors looking on – well, I just can't face it. No, I – I – I simply can't face it.

MR. CARTER: (*grimly*) You can't back out, Wilkins. The show must go on. Perhaps Mr. Borrowmore won't turn up till you've finished your part. After all, it won't take long, judging by how much you know of it!

MR. WILKINS: I – I – Corwumph!

MR. CARTER: Well, I must get along into the hall and keep an eye on the audience. (*going*) Good luck, Wilkins.

Door opens

(*at door*) Oh, hullo, Jennings. My word, that's a smart costume!

JENNINGS: (*at door*) Yes, sir. May I speak to Mr. Wilkins, sir. It's urgent.

MR. CARTER: (*going*) Yes, go along in, Jennings.

Door closes

JENNINGS: (*approaching*) Sir, Mr. Wilkins, sir.

MR. WILKINS: What is it, Jennings?

JENNINGS: Well, sir, I'm terribly sorry, but we've made a bit of a bish about your costume, sir, and...

MR. WILKINS: *Costume!* You don't mean you're expecting me to *dress up* for this ghastly charade, do you?

JENNINGS: Yes, of course, sir. We all are. But the only thing I can find for you is this red blanket and this coal scuttle to put on your head, sir.

MR. WILKINS: I – I – Corwumph! I'm not going on wearing any trumpery household furniture, and don't you think it!

JENNINGS: Oh, please, sir. We're all ready to start.

MR. WILKINS: I never heard such ridiculous nonsense in my life! It's preposterous! It's the last straw! No, Jennings, I positively refuse to march on to the stage in front of the whole school wearing a dirty brass coal scuttle smothered in coal dust. It's all off, you understand. I am *not* going to perform.

JENNINGS: Oh, but, sir, please! And after you've taken the trouble to learn your speech.

MR. WILKINS: I – I... You heard what I said, Jennings. I suggest you go and ask Mr. Carter to announce that the concert has had to be cancelled. And that's my last word.

JENNINGS: (*distressed*) Yes, sir.

Footsteps to door, door opens/shuts

(*at microphone: distressed: in tears*) Oh, heavens! Oh, golly! What on earth can I do? What on *earth* can I do?

IRVING B: (*approaching*) What can you do, sonny? Well, for a start you can tell me where I'm supposed to get ready for my performance.

JENNINGS: Oh, you made me jump. Who are you, please?

IRVING: Who am I?   Does the name Irving Borrowmore convey anything to you?

JENNINGS: No, I'm afraid it doesn't.

IRVING B: Pity! I had hoped I was better known, but no matter. Tell me, why do you wear a cardboard chest-protector and strip-metal shin-pads? Is it a new fashion?

JENNINGS: No; it's my armour-plating.

IRVING B: Ah, yes. A very useful precaution when paying a visit to the headmaster's study. I remember when I was at school, a couple of exercise books, judiciously placed... what?

JENNINGS: Oh, no, it's nothing like that. I'm wearing my armour because we were going to do a hunk out of Henry V, but now Mr. Wilkins has spoilt it all and won't take part, just because he's only got a coal-scuttle for a helmet.

IRVING B: And that is why you appear so distressed?

JENNINGS: Well, so would anyone be. I just don't know what to do. The audience are all sitting there waiting and Matron's made these smashing costumes, and there's been a rumour going round that it was going to be a really decent show with a special surprise person playing King Henry.

IRVING B: Sad; very sad. H'm. Which part of the play were you hoping to perform?

JENNINGS: Only a short bit; that scene before the battle of Agincourt where he comes on and talks about the feast of Crispian – if you know the bit I mean.

IRVING B: Indeed, I do, sonny. Indeed, I do.
"This day is called the feast of Crispian,
He that outlives this day, and comes safe home,
Will stand a-tip-toe when this day is named,
And rouse him at the name of Crispian.
He that shall live this day and see old age
Will yearly on the vigil feast his neighbours,
And say 'Tomorrow is Saint Crispian'... "

JENNINGS: Wow! I say! Why, you're even better than Mr. Wilkins. Fancy you knowing all that speech off by heart.

IRVING B: Hardly surprising, dear boy, considering that I've come here specially to recite it. It forms one of the items of my repertoire.

JENNINGS: Does it! Oh, wacko! I say, would you be awfully decent and go on and do it now, in our play? Everything's all ready, and here's the coal scuttle and the red blanket. They're not much to look at, but...

IRVING B: *Not* the coal scuttle, thank you; *nor* the red blanket. I have something a little more suitable here in my bag.

Suitcase opened

JENNINGS: Wow! Real armour! Proper chain-mail and a silver helmet! I say, sir, it'd be wonderful if you'd really play King Henry for us. Will you? You can change in this little room here, look.

IRVING B: Fair enough, dear boy. Give me a minute or two to get ready; then let the curtain rise on Agincourt.

JENNINGS: I'll just go and tell the other chaps to stand by. Talk about a surprise for the audience. This is going to knock the cast for six, as well!

Fade. Fade in distant sound of audience in hall.

Microphone is in the wings

TEMPLE: Well, I don't know about you, Venables, but I wish I'd never said I'd be in this rotten play at all. It's going to be an awful bish, if you ask me.

VENABLES: I know, I know. If only we could get started. I've just had a peep through the curtains and the chaps in the front row are getting as fidgety as blinko. What on earth can have happened to Jennings?

DARBISHIRE: (*turning*) Here he is, coming now... I say, Jen, what's gone wrong? We're hours late starting.

JENNINGS: (*approaching*) It's all right, Darbishire. I had a spot of bother with Mr. Wilkins. He refuses to go on.

OMNES: What! Oh gosh, no!

DARBISHIRE: This is ghastly! Whatever are we going to do? The hall's just bursting with chaps all panting for us to start. They're expecting a big surprise, too.

ATKINSON: They'll get that all right, when no one comes on.

JENNINGS: No, no, it's all right. Don't get in a flap. I've fixed everything up with the proper Henry V. He's going to take his place.

VENABLES: You're crazy! He's been dead about five hundred years.

JENNINGS: That's all part of the surprise. You chaps are in for a shock.

TEMPLE: We've just had it, haven't we? Oh fish-hooks, I wish I wasn't in this play!

JENNINGS: Blow your fanfare, Darbi. We're all ready to start.

DARBISHIRE: How *can* we be ready when we haven't got the leading man..?

JENNINGS: Oh, go *on*, Darbishire. Do as I tell you.

DARBISHIRE: (*going*) Okay. But I'm not taking the blame if everyone boos and hisses.

Increase atmosphere of hall a little. Microphone is now in hall.

Down atmosphere to silence during fanfare.

Fanfare on trumpet, mild applause.

VENABLES: *"Where is the king?"*

ATKINSON: *"The king himself is rode to view the battle."*

DARBISHIRE: *"Of fighting men they have full threescore thousand."*

TEMPLE: *"There's five to one; beside they all are fresh."*

DARBISHIRE: (*whispers at mic*)
Oh goodness, Venables, I'm trembling like a brace of jellies. What on earth's going to happen?

VENABLES: I don't know, Darbi. I expect they'll start booing when it goes wrong. I reckon Jennings must be stark raving crackers.

DARBISHIRE: We're getting nearer and nearer to King Henry's entrance. And then what?

JENNINGS: (*background*)
"God's arm strike with us!
'Tis a fearful odds.
God be with you, princes all,
I'll to my charge.
If we meet no more till we meet in heaven,
Then joyfully – my noble Lord of Bedford,
My dear Lord Gloucester –
and my good Lord Exeter
And my kind kinsman,
warriors all,
adieu."

ATKINSON: *"Farewell, good Salisbury; and good luck go with thee."*

TEMPLE: *"Farewell kind lord; fight valiantly today;*
And yet I do thee wrong to mind thee of it.
For thou art framed of the firm truth of valour."

DARBISHIRE: *"Oh, that we now had here*
But one ten thousand of those men in England
That do no work today."

IRVING B: (*approaching*) *"What's he that wishes so?*
My cousin Westmoreland? No my fair cousin."

DARBISHIRE: (*close*) Heavens! Who's this? Where's he come from?

VENABLES: (*close*) Petrified paintpots! It really *is* Henry V!

IRVING B: *"If we are markt to die, we are enow*
To do our country loss; and if to live,
The fewer men, the greater share of honour.
God's will! I pray thee, wish not one man more.
By jove, I am not covetous for gold;
Nor care I who doth feed upon my cost."

Fade down/up

"And Crispin Crispian shall ne'er go by
From this day to the ending of the world
But we in it shall be remembered –
We few, we happy few, we band of brothers;
For he today that sheds his blood with me
Shall be my brother; be he ne'er so vile,
This day shall gentle his condition;
And gentlemen in England now a-bed
Shall think themselves accurst they were not here;
And hold their manhoods cheap whiles any speaks
That fought with us upon Saint Crispin's day!"

Loud applause. Fade down, then up again to background

OMNES: Wizard show, wasn't it! Smashing! Wasn't Henry V supersonic!

DARBISHIRE: Ssh! Quiet; Mr. Carter's going to say something.

Applause dies to silence

MR. CARTER: Ladies and gentlemen: this has been a most successful concert which we've all enjoyed very much.

MR. WILKINS: (*loudly*) Hear, hear. Hear, hear.

Appreciation from audience in background: dies

MR. CARTER: We must remember the people who have worked hard to entertain us – Matron for making these splendid costumes; Jennings and his company of heavily armoured barons; and, of course, Mr. Irving Borrowmore for acting on King Henry V's inspired orders and stepping into the breach with seconds to spare.

Laughter

Nor must we forget to thank Mr. Wilkins who so modestly stepped *out* of the breach so that Mr. Borrowmore could step *into* it.

Cheers and applause

Well, it's almost over now – our little concert to mark the close of another term; so before we go upstairs for the last time, let us give three hearty cheers: one for the term's hard work, one for the concert which brings it to an end, and last and loudest, one for the holidays. Hip, hip...

Fade out on cheers.

WHILE I REMEMBER
the Autobiography
of
ANTHONY BUCKERIDGE

Anthony Buckeridge shot to fame with his radio plays about the fictional schoolboy Jennings, whose adventures in book form have delighted millions of readers around the world. In this autobiography, not only does Buckeridge tell us of the origins of this much-loved character, but he describes a varied and often fascinating life. It begins with his description of the horrific death of his father and moves on through his tough education, his work first in banking and then in teaching, his fascination for the world of theatre, and of course his writing. Buckeridge has produced a heartfelt story which will be as engrossing and entertaining for his countless fans as the fictional exploits of Jennings, Rex Milligan and the Bligh family have been for over 50 years.

David Bathurst, author of *The Jennings Companion*, prefaces the book with a brief sequel to the Companion, and provides an appendix giving some background to the illustrators of the Jennings stories.

Published by David Schutte in softback, A5 size, 96 pages
£10 + £1 postage, ISBN 0 9521482 1 8

DS
David Schutte
119 Sussex Road, Petersfield, Hampshire GU31 4LB
Telephone: 01730 269115 Fax: 231177

JENNINGS SOUNDS THE ALARM
seven plays for radio
by
ANTHONY BUCKERIDGE

Illustrated by Val Biro

With the majority of the original BBC radio recordings of the Jennings plays lost forever, it was great news when Anthony Buckeridge agreed to the publication of the original manuscripts in book form so that they could be enjoyed by his countless fans for years to come. The plays in this first volume have been lovingly and delightfully illustrated by Val Biro, best known for his series of books on Gumdrop, the vintage car. He also illustrated the dustwrapper and frontispiece for the first edition of *Typically Jennings* in 1971.

The first Jennings play, *Jennings Learns the Ropes*, was broadcast on the Home Service for Children's Hour on 6th October 1948, and was followed *by Jennings and the Poisonous Spider, Jennings and the Friend of the Family, Jennings Sees the Light, Jennings and the Very Important Parent, Jennings and the Unwelcome Gift*, and, for Request Week on 5th April 1949, *Jennings Sounds the Alarm*.

More volumes will follow until all 62 plays have been published.

Published by David Schutte in softback, A5 size, 176 pages
£12.00 + £1 postage, ISBN 0 9521482 2 6

DS
David Schutte
119 Sussex Road, Petersfield, Hampshire GU31 4LB
Telephone: 01730 269115 Fax: 231177

JENNINGS BREAKS THE RECORD
seven more plays for radio
by
ANTHONY BUCKERIDGE

Illustrated by Val Biro

Petrified Plutonium!

Will a broken back brake block break Jennings' journey? Could the mad scientist in the woods succeed in blowing up Sussex? What will become of Darbishire's idea for a Society for the Prevention of Cruelty to Crocodiles on Sundays?

These questions and others can only be answered by reading this second volume of Jennings' adventures on radio, published for the first time. Here you will find seven more of the original scripts, exactly as they were broadcast 50 years ago when *Jennings at School* established itself as one of the most popular radio programmes ever on the BBC's *Children's Hour*.

With Val Biro's charming illustrations to complement Anthony Buckeridge's tales of Linbury Court School, this is a book that will delight Jennings' fans young and old, the world over.

More volumes will follow until all 62 plays have been published.

Published by David Schutte in softback, A5 size, 176 pages
£12.00 + £1 postage, ISBN 0 9521482 3 4

DS
David Schutte
119 Sussex Road, Petersfield, Hampshire GU31 4LB
Telephone: 01730 269115 Fax: 231177

JENNINGS JOINS THE SEARCH PARTY
Plays for radio - volume 3
by
ANTHONY BUCKERIDGE

Illustrated by Val Biro

Jumping Jellyfish!

Can Jennings and Darbishire plod homeward before the curfew tolls the knell of parting day, or will they be stuck in Pottlewhistle Halt for ever? Will their *Flixton Slick - Super Sleuth* become a classic of modern literature? Should L.P. Wilkins Esq. give in to blackmail when his sister threatens to spill the beans about his initials? Under what circumstances does Darbishire resemble a pumpkin in a peanut shell?

More intriguing questions from the world of J.C.T.Jennings can be found in this third volume of original *Jennings at School* scripts, introduced and illustrated by Val Biro. They are now published for the first time, exactly as they were broadcast 50 years ago, confirming Anthony Buckeridge's reputation as one of the most popular writers ever for the BBC's *Children's Hour.*

More volumes will follow until all 62 plays have been published.

Published by David Schutte in softback, A5 size, 160 pages
£12.00 + £1 postage, ISBN 0 9521482 4 2

DS
David Schutte
119 Sussex Road, Petersfield, Hampshire GU31 4LB
Telephone: 01730 269115 Fax: 231177

JENNINGS AND THE ROMAN REMAINS

Plays for radio – volume 5
by
ANTHONY BUCKERIDGE

Illustrated by Val Biro

Corwumph!

Why is a disused wheel once belonging to a Linbury Corporation dust-cart being exhibited between a fragment of fourth century hypocaust and the spear of a Roman centurion? Wherein lies Jennings' main objection to Panama Pete of Dead Man's Gulch? What is the French for "What is this that this is that that" and when is it best to use it? Can Jennings' piano playing acquire a smoothness of touch when his fingers are smeared with a sticky mixture of toffee and plasticine?

Here in the fifth volume are another six episodes from the original *Jennings at School* radio series, first broadcast in the early 1950s on the BBC's *Children's Hour*. Sadly, only a few of the original recordings have survived, but here are the scripts, exactly as written, for fans and future generations to enjoy.

More volumes will follow until all 62 plays have been published.

Published by David Schutte in softback, A5 size, 144 pages
£12.00 + £1 postage, ISBN 0 9521482 6 9

DS
David Schutte
119 Sussex Road, Petersfield, Hampshire GU31 4LB
Telephone: 01730 269115 Fax: 231177

INTRODUCING REX MILLIGAN

By

ANTHONY BUCKERIDGE

Illustrated by Val Biro

Rex Milligan made his bow in a short story entitled *Introducing Rex Milligan* on 12th October 1951 in *Eagle* comic - just over 50 years ago. More stories followed, then the first full-length book was serialised - *Rex Milligan's Busy Term (1953).*

Three more Milligan books followed, all published by Lutterworth Press: *Rex Milligan Raises the Roof* (1955), *Rex Milligan Holds Forth* (1957), and *Rex Milligan Reporting* (1961), but sixteen of those original stories in the *Eagle* never found their way into a book.

Until now!

Now at last, after a short delay of half a century, you can enjoy the humour of Anthony Buckeridge's other schoolboy hero in these classic long-lost stories.

Anthony Buckeridge himself has written a short introduction to the book, which is published to celebrate his 90th birthday in June 2002.

Published by David Schutte in softback, A5 size, 160 pages
£12.00 + £1 postage, ISBN 0 9521482 7 7

DS

David Schutte
119 Sussex Road, Petersfield, Hampshire GU31 4LB
Telephone: 01730 269115 Fax: 231177